LOUIS WALSH'S
FAST TRACK TO FAME

The A – Z Guide to Superstardom

Louis Walsh

BANTAM PRESS

LONDON · TORONTO · SYDNEY · AUCKLAND · JOHANNESBURG

CONTENTS

LOUIS WALSH'S
FAST TRACK TO FAME

www.**rbooks**.co.uk

PICTURE ACKNOWLEDGEMENTS

5: Getty Images; 6: © Neal Preston/Corbis; 9: ITV/Rex Features;
10–11: Ken McKay/Rex Features; 13: © Len Prince/JBG Idols;
14:Cathal McNaughton/PA Archive/PA Photos; 15: Sky Brackpool/Rex
Features; 16: © Bettmann/Corbis; 18: Getty Images; 20: Reuters/Corbis;
23: © Mario Anzuoni/Reuters/Corbis; 24: © Philip Ollerenshaw/Idols;
25: Michel Linssen/Redferns; 27: Rex Features; 28–9: © Ethan Miller/
Corbis; 31: © Reuters/Corbis; 32: © Perou/Idols; 33: © Lynn Goldsmith/
Corbis; 35: © David Venni/Idols; 36–7: © Philip Ollerenshaw/Idols;
38: © Tim Roney/Idols; 39: Julian Makey/Rex Features; 42: © WWD/
Condé Nast/Corbis; 43: © Ulf Magnusson/Idols; 45: © Sacha Waldman/
Idols; 48: © Stephanie Cardinale/Corbis; 51: © Daniel Deme/epa/
Corbis; 52 © Roland Wehlrauch/dpa/Corbis; 55: © S. I. N. /Corbis;
56–7: Suzan/EMPICS Entertainment/PA Photos; 58: Getty Images;
62: Getty Images; 65: © Albert Ferreira/Reuters/Corbis; 67: © Peter M.
Fisher/Corbis; 68: © Reuters/Corbis; 70: Tim Wimborne/Reuters/Corbis;
73: Ferdaus Shamin/Sygma/Corbis; 74–5: Chapman/Rex Features;
76: © Reuters/Corbis; 78: © Scott McDermott/Corbis; 79: © Eric
Gaillard/Reuters/Corbis; 81: © Rune Hellestad/Corbis; 82–3: © William
Rutten/Idols; 85: © Marc Brasz/Corbis; 86–7: Getty Images; 89: Ken
McKay/Rex Features; 90–91: © Tracy Bayne/Shooting Star/Idols;
92: © Neal Preston/Idols; 93: Ken McKay/ Features; 95: © Tim
Mosenfelde/Corbis; 96: © Rune Hellestad/Corbis; 98: © Roger Sargent/
Idols; 100–101: © Stephanie Cardinale/People Avenue/Corbis;
103: © Nitin Vadukul/Idols; 107: © Corbis/Sygma; 111: © Reuters/
Corbis; 112: Tim Ockenden/PA Archive/PA Photos; 116: Getty Images;
120: Getty Images; 123: Getty Images; 124: © Tim Mosenfelder/
Corbis; 126–7: © S.I.N./Corbis; 129: © Dylan Martinez/Reuters/Corbis;
130–131: Getty Images/WireImage; 132: Brian Rasic/Rex Features;
133: © Ulf Magnusson/Idols; 134: David Fisher/Rex Features;
136: © Steve Azzara/Corbis; 137: Matthew Fearn/PA Archive/PA Photos;
138: Mousse/ABACA/PA Photos; 141: © Reuters/Corbis; 142: © Reuters/
Corbis; 145: © Tom Roney/Idols; 146: Everett Collection: Rex Features;
147: Brian Rasic/Rex Features; 149: Brian Rasic/Rex Features;
151: © Susanna Vera/Reuters/Corbis; 152–3: © Everett Kennedy
Brown/epa/Corbis; 154: Rune Hellestad/Corbis; 155: Yui Mok/PA Wire/PA
Photos; 156:© Firooz Zahedi/JGB Idols; 161: © Mark S. Wexler/Corbis;
163: Getty Images; 164 *top*: © Jeff Minton/Corbis; 164 *btm*: © Christopher
Morris/Corbis; 165: © Peter Turnley/Corbis; 166: Getty Images;
167: © Danielle La Monaca/Reuters/Corbis; 168: Gustavo Bom/AP/PA
Photos; 173: Rex Features; 175: Ken McKay/Rex Features;
177: Rex Features; 178–80: © Michelle Pedone/zefa/Corbis; 180: Getty
Images; 181: © Frank Trapper /Corbis Sygma; 183: © Thomas Rabsch/
Idols; 184: © Markus Stuecklin/epa/Corbis; 186: © Neal Preston/Corbis;
187: © Neal Preston/Corbis; 188 top: © Stephanie Cardinale/People
Avenue/Corbis; 188–9: © Envision/Corbis; 189: © Tom Howard/Idols;
190: © Reuters/Corbis; 192: © Lucy Nicholson/Reuters/Corbis;
194–5: © Reuters/Corbis; 196: © Neal Preston/Corbis; 197: © Rune
Hellestad/Corbis; 199: © Jim Ruymen/Reuters/Corbis;
200–201: © Mario Anzuoni/Reuters/Corbis; 202: P. Anastasselis/Rex
Features; 203: © Mario Anzuoni/Reuters/Corbis; 204: © David Venni/
Idols; © Content Mine International/Alamy; 206: © 2002/Topham/AP;
207: © Reuters/Corbis; 208: © Stephanie Cardinale/Corbis; 210: Michel
Ponomareff/Rex Features; 211: © Redferns Music Picture Library/Alamy;
212–13: © Redferns Music Picture Library/Alamy; 214–15: Skyline/Rex
Features; 216: Ken McKay/Rex Features; 217: WireImage/Getty Images;
218: © Barry J. Holmes/LaMoine Photo Group/Idols; 221: Getty
Images; 224: Getty Images; 230–31: Ken McKay/Rex Features; 232: Ken
McKay/Rex Features; 234: Ken McKay/Rex Features; 236: Ken McKay/
Rex Features; 237: Ian West/PA Archive/PA Photos; 238: Ken McKay/Rex
Features; 241: Ken McKay/Rex Features; 242–3: Getty Images;
244: epa/Corbis; 245: Julien Behal/PA Wire/PA Photos; 246–7: ITV/Rex
Features; 248: Tim Rooke/Rex Features; 249: Getty Images; 251: Ken
McKay; 252: © Rune Hellestad/Corbis; 254: courtesy Priscilla Samuels;
255: © S.I.N./Corbis.

TRANSWORLD PUBLISHERS
61–63 Uxbridge Road, London W5 5SA
A Random House Group Company
www.booksattransworld.co.uk

First published in Great Britain
in 2007 by Bantam Press
an imprint of Transworld Publishers

Copyright © Louis Walsh and Kathryn Rogers
2007

Louis Walsh and Kathryn Rogers have asserted
their right under the Copyright, Designs and
Patents Act 1988 to be identified as the authors
of this work.

A CIP catalogue record for this book
is available from the British Library.

ISBNs 9780593059012 (cased)
9780593059647 (tpb)

Addresses for Random House Group Ltd
companies outside the UK can be found at:
www.randomhouse.co.uk
The Random House Group Ltd
Reg. No. 954009

The Random House Group Ltd makes every effort
to ensure that the papers used in its books are
made from trees that have been legally sourced
from well-managed and credibly certified forests.
Our paper procurement policy can be found at:
www.randomhouse.co.uk/paper.htm

Typeset in Trade Gothic
Printed in Germany

2 4 6 8 10 9 7 5 3 1

FOREWORD

I HAD NEVER heard of Louis Walsh until he wrote a scathing personal attack on my daughter Kelly in a magazine. It was a good thing I was on a different continent at the time!

By the time I met him, on the very first *X Factor* show, Louis had apologized profusely and I was ready to give him the benefit of the doubt. On the first day we talked, on the second day we laughed, and we haven't stopped talking and laughing since! He's the wonderful antithesis to the typical slick, loud and sleazy American manager. He has an unexpected child-like giddiness about him and always has a twinkle in his eye, ready for mischief at every opportunity – just like a naughty schoolboy. He's the best gossip and we speak to each other day or night as there's always something going on.

Don't let his charm fool you, though, because behind all the smiles and laughter Louis has a tough and ambitious streak, which has led to his consistent success and also to *Music Week* naming him as one of the top fifty most influential people in the UK music industry.

If it appeared that Louis shattered some dreams while we worked on *X Factor*, this was sometimes for the best. The music business is unforgiving and there are times when you have to be cruel to be kind in order to save someone from even more heartache further down the line.

If I have learned anything over the three years I've spent on *X Factor* with Louis, it's never to underestimate this Irishman. He has an incredible knowledge of music and knows every writer and producer of every song across all the genres. If ever we were stuck for a song choice for our artists on the show, Louis would always come up with the right suggestion.

He is responsible for creating two of the biggest boybands in the industry – Boyzone and Westlife. Boyzone had nine Number 1 singles and sold eleven million albums before Louis really got into his stride. Westlife have so far had fourteen Number 1 hits, and album sales in excess of forty million. If this wasn't enough, he's also the star-maker behind hit acts such as Shayne Ward, Girls Aloud, G4, Ronan Keating and Samantha Mumba. He even masterminded Lulu's chart comeback a few years ago with an ITV tribute show and album of duets, including performances by Paul McCartney, Sting and Elton John. It was Lulu's most successful album release ever.

Louis is naturally insightful, intuitive and funny, and surrounds himself with really nice people, which is very telling of his own character. He's also fiercely loyal and extremely passionate about his artists; a rare quality these days.

This man is a treasured and good friend to me and I am very lucky to have him in my life.

Sharon Osbourne

THE SUCCESS OF stars from Girls Aloud to Justin Timberlake makes the world of pop and rock seem like a good career move. Limousines, private planes, fast cars, designer clothes and five-star hotels are the trappings of a pop star's lifestyle. So it's not surprising that every day of the week I'm approached by aspiring young musicians. They press their demos into my hands in the hope that I'm going to make their wildest pop dreams come true. Or they audition before me in the hope that they'll be catapulted to fame and fortune. **Sometimes I can see or hear definite potential in an act. Yet I know they're never going to make it. Only the ones that stand head and shoulders above the rest will get the break. Most of the others scupper their chances because of inexperience, naivety and laziness.** This is why the road to success in the music business is littered with more pop flops than superstars. And this is where *Fast Track to Fame* comes in.

Nobody in the music business can nurse every promising artist they come across. After all, there are a lot of would-be stars out there. *Fast Track* aims to teach you how to stand out from the crowd, to become the success you've always dreamed of being.

This book contains everything I wish I'd known when I was starting out. It took many years of hard work gaining experience before I managed to unlock many of the secrets of success in this business. As a result, I've been able to steer Shayne Ward, Westlife, Girls Aloud, Boyzone, Ronan Keating, G4 and Samantha Mumba to the heady heights of pop stardom. But, it wasn't easy. There are lots of paths to the top of every mountain, and it's fair to say I took one of the longest and rockiest routes.

There were several years when record companies wouldn't take my calls. There were occasions when my artists had smaller audiences than those you'd see in the toilets at a Westlife concert. And there were lots of times when I was completely and utterly broke. I was never disheartened enough to give up, but if I'd known then what I know now, I would have found my way with a lot less heartache.

Hopefully, with the help of this book, you won't have to learn everything the hard way like I did. After all, cracking the music industry is not easy, but why make it harder than it needs to be? The truth is that you have to display star quality before anyone in the industry will take a chance on you. It costs millions to launch an artist, so you have to look as though you're worth it; you have to stand out from the thousands of wannabes out there and show that you have that something special, that star quality, that X factor.

This book aims to help you to become that someone special and gives you the practical information you need to get that edge on the competition. I also hope it provides many thought-provoking ideas and inspiring tales from someone who knows and loves the music industry. That would be me.

> *Nobody trips over mountains. It is the small pebble that causes you to stumble.*
>
> Proverb

So, do you still want to be a pop star? Join me then on this **Fast Track to Fame**...

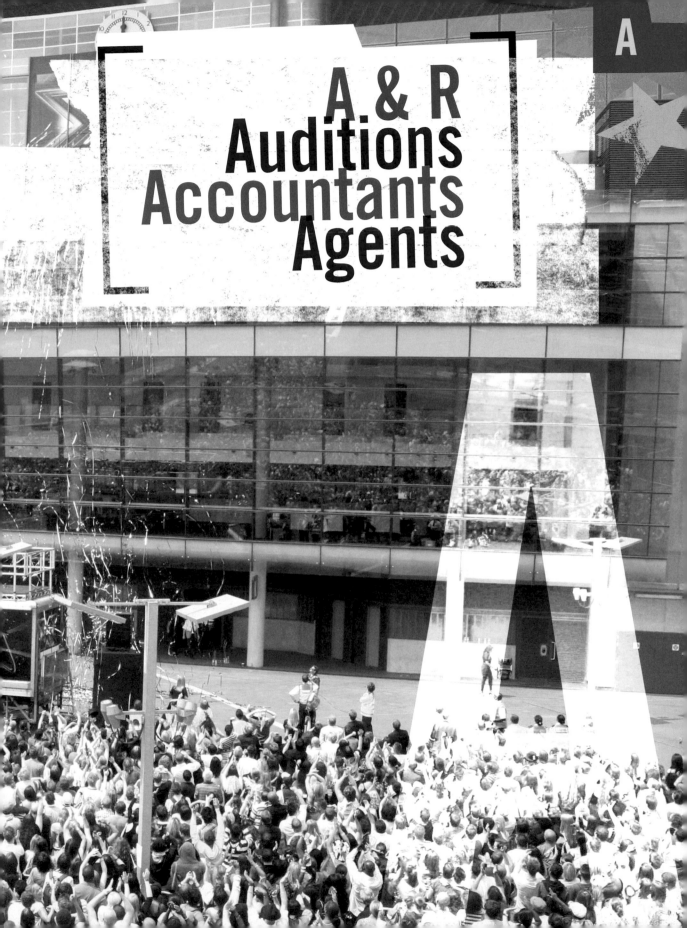

A & R
Auditions
Accountants
Agents

MR MUSIC MAN AND WOMAN

> *Trying to get an opinion from an A&R guy is like trying to get blood out of a stone!*
>
> Vivian Campbell, guitarist with Def Leppard

VIVIAN CAMPBELL AND Jewel have no great love for A&Rs, and they aren't alone. A&R stands for Artists and Repertoire; they are the scouts of the music industry, who are always under pressure to find new talent.

A&R people work in both record companies and music publishers. Those working in the former are looking for new artists and hit records; those in the latter are seeking talented songwriters and hit songs. Remember: if they're not successful, their jobs are on the line. So how do they minimize the risk of losing their jobs? Many of them don't take chances. The possibility that they'll sign you purely on the fact that your brilliant demo has landed on their desk is about as likely as winning the lotto. The A&R is only interested in those who are already generating a buzz on the music scene.

They want to hear word of mouth from DJs or producers. They want to see reviews in the music press. They want to find an act that has just been signed by a reputable manager, an act that people are already talking about and that already has an audience. What an A&R really, really wants is a sure thing. If they can't get that, then they want a fairly sure thing. They will only bring what they see as a safe bet to the record company's attention. There are probably around 500 A&Rs in record companies and music publishers around the UK and Ireland. However, only a handful of them are truly successful.

WHAT DOES A RECORD COMPANY A&R DO?

An A&R person finds the artists that are signed by the record companies. He or she listens to demos, goes to gigs and tries to stay on top of rapidly changing music tastes and fads. They keep their ear to the ground, listening for a buzz about new acts; they keep an eye on the internet, and pore over music and style magazines such as *NME*, *i-D*, *Hit Sheet* and *Dazed & Confused*. Their job is to sign 'The Next Big Thing'.

Once an artist is signed by a record company, the A&R person is also the bridge between them and the label. The A&R sorts out the record deal and is then heavily involved in the recording of the début album.

A&R people have to be passionate about music. They are often music anoraks who come to the attention of record companies because of their knowledge of the live music scene. Many start off working in specialist record stores or as DJs, and have an intimate

> *A&Rs generally have no ears. In general they're all young schmucks who are looking for something to copy – whatever is big. They don't really have much foresight.*
>
> Jewel

knowledge of 'white labels'. In the early days of dance music, white labels referred to twelve-inch vinyl records, which contained limited information about the artist on the plain white cover. Sometimes this was because they had illegally sampled or remixed copyright music, and sometimes it was just because it was considered 'cool'. These white labels were issued to create an advance buzz. Today, white labels can be any record or song – whether it's an MP3, CD or vinyl – that's not issued by a record label. They are usually distributed to DJs and small record stores as promotional devices and to test the market. If your white label takes off in the clubs or on pirate radio, you've a good chance of coming to the attention of an A&R and getting a commercial release.

An A&R just starting out can be paid as little as £20,000 for long working hours. Yet if they become as successful as Clive Davis in America or Simon Cowell in the UK, they can expect salaries of hundreds of thousands, possibly millions of pounds.

A&R HEAVEN: THE LIGHTHOUSE FAMILY

Sometimes a record deal can fall like manna from heaven. Colin Barlow, a former A&R, who is now the head of Polydor Records, recalls how he snapped up The Lighthouse Family.

'That was the maddest signing I ever did,' he says. 'I took an unsolicited call from someone who said he wanted to play me a song down the phone. I don't know how I ended up taking this call – I probably thought "this will take thirty seconds, just do it and get it over with." He played "Ocean Drive" by The Lighthouse Family. I took a complete punt and drove to Newcastle to see them straight away. It never happened before or since. I just heard this song for thirty seconds and thought "this is too good to be true!".'

It turned out to be a good punt: The Lighthouse Family's début album *Ocean Drive* sold 1.6 million copies and they became one of the big success stories of the nineties.

A&R HELL: SAMANTHA MUMBA

Singer Samantha Mumba should have had the pop world at her feet by now. She went to the top of the Billboard charts in America when no one on this side of the world could achieve it. She's got star quality and talent, but things didn't go according to plan. She was originally signed by Polydor's Colin Barlow and, like me, he's still frustrated about the one that got away.

'Samantha was an incredible success story,' he says. 'We signed her as a fifteen-year-old girl. We did everything right and she had a Number 1 hit in America with her début single "Gotta Tell You". We put it to radio there and it just took off. Our big mistake was letting the Americans take over.'

He explains: 'We hadn't dealt with the big American egos like this before. We thought they knew what they were talking about. Instead they took this really special talent and made her sound like everyone else. They changed everything that made her special and turned her into another clone. It was really frustrating to watch it happen.'

We'll be seeing even more of Samantha Mumba in the future!

Samantha never got to release a second album. She hasn't had a record deal since late 2003. I tried finding her another deal in the UK, but it's difficult to get any female artist signed these days. She moved to the United States in 2005 and has been working on recording new material ever since. Her most recent and very public effort to resurrect her career was in April 2007 with the Channel 4 show *Get Your Act Together*. The programme followed promoter Harvey Goldsmith's attempts to get Samantha a record deal. They staged a showcase for the UK record industry, and Samantha performed live at La Pigalle club in London. The programme didn't do her any favours – she came across as a bit of a prima donna, turning up late for meetings and not taking Harvey's advice. I think this reality TV experience backfired spectacularly for her, but I still don't think we've seen the last of Ms Mumba. She's ambitious, talented and will see this as just a temporary setback in her young life.

TOP A&Rs
Here's a few of the best in the business.

Simon Cowell
Simon Cowell is one of the most successful pop A&R guys in the UK because he has a really commercial ear and knows a hit as soon as he hears it. He's signed acts such as Sinitta, Robson & Jerome, Westlife, Five, Zig & Zag, Gareth Gates, Will Young and all the *X Factor* winners.

Colin Barlow
Another one of the greats is Colin Barlow, who is now head man at Polydor. He signed many of my acts, including Boyzone and Girls Aloud.

Jamie Nelson
Jamie Nelson of Parlophone Records is another top class A&R, with blue-chip signings including Kylie Minogue, Jamelia, Lily Allen, Simon Webbe and Beverley Knight.

Chris Briggs
EMI's legendary Chris Briggs is an A&R at the top of his game, and a gentleman to boot. He signed the great showman Robbie Williams, and Geri Halliwell among many others.

Clive Davis
The undisputed king of A&Rs is Clive Davis, who now runs J Records in America. He's a legendary record breaker, with acts such as Barry Manilow, Billy Joel, Bruce Springsteen, Chicago, Whitney Houston and Alicia Keys. He also signs all the *American Pop Idol* successes and is taking *X Factor* winner Leona Lewis to the US. If he can't help her break the market there, no one can.

FAST TRACK TO FINDING A&Rs

Music industry directories such as *The Unsigned Guide* contain listings of A&Rs. See D for Directories for details.

A&R people worldwide are featured on **www.hitquarters.com**, along with the acts they've broken. This is a subscription site and you have to pay $15 if you want to access their contact details. Still, once you have the name of the act and the A&R person, it's quite easy to find the record company and get the contact details yourself elsewhere.

You can also call a record company that specializes in your style of music and get the name of their A&R person. It's probably a good idea to call anyway because people move on to new jobs and companies, and directory details can become out of date very quickly. See D for Demos and P for Press Pack to find out how to introduce yourself to A&Rs.

ACCOUNTANTS
MUSIC'S BEAN COUNTERS

> *I have no use for bodyguards, but I have very specific use for two highly trained certified public accountants.*
>
> Elvis Presley

DESPITE HIS RELIANCE on accountants, Elvis was either not getting good advice or not taking that advice. When he died in 1977, the most successful artist in music history was on the verge of bankruptcy.

Even the biggest artists can end up broke because of swindling managers or record companies. It's unusual for this to happen in the UK any more, as artists usually deal directly with an accountant and a lawyer, and you would have to be very unlucky to be defrauded by these professionals. However, it does still happen in America, where artists tend to leave the intricacies of their finances to 'business managers', who are separate from their day-to-day music managers.

I know it doesn't sound very exciting, but a music accountant is an essential part of a successful artist's team. He will deal with your income and royalties and also with your tax payments.

You should get yourself an accountant as soon as you have an income or are offered a record deal. No matter how implicitly you trust your manager or your A&R, it is important to get independent financial advice at this stage. After all, eighties pop artist Samantha Fox claimed her manager swindled her out of a fortune, and he was her dad! LeAnn Rimes and her dad, Wilbur, also ended up in a bitter feud over financial issues, some years ago.

It's also important to find an accountant who understands or specializes in the music business. Look for recommendations. The music business is quite a small one and reputation stands for everything. If an accountant is seen to be doing anything underhand or is not up to scratch, word will get around fast.

Find an accountant who is already working with successful acts. Under the terms of your record and managerial contract, he or she should have the right to audit your record company, manager or publisher every few years. Remember that auditing is a serious business and it doesn't come cheap. The only time an artist will call upon an accountant to perform an audit is if they suspect they are being seriously defrauded of earnings.

HOW MUCH DOES AN ACCOUNTANT COST?

Successful artists will pay for their number crunchers' services by the hour. The mid-range charge for accountants looking after general accounts and tax returns is around £50 per hour; juniors charge £30 per hour.

More experienced music accountants or senior partners may be required for overseeing commercial work or important financial negotiations for an artist. They can charge £200 per hour for the privilege. Irish accountants usually charge the same figure in euros, and so are considerably cheaper. If you are an emerging artist and just want your tax return sorted out, find an accountant who will charge a flat fee.

FAST TRACK TO DIY TAX RETURNS

If money is still too tight to mention, keep a record of your income and your outgoing expenditure, and file your own tax return. There are numerous expenses you can legitimately claim as a self-employed artist – everything from music publications to leads, plugs and transportation.

You can get all the details on your entitlements and responsibilities from the Inland Revenue in the UK at **www.hmrc.gov.uk**; or the Irish Revenue in Ireland at **www.revenue.ie**.

FAST TRACK TO FINDING A MUSIC ACCOUNTANT

Contact the Association of Music Industry Accountants (AMIA) in the UK at 66 Chiltern Street, London W1U 4JT; phone (020) 7535 1400.

Also try Alan McEvoy at Live Wire Business, which has offices in London and Limerick. He worked with the Cranberries and works with all my acts, including Westlife, Ronan Keating, Shayne Ward and Girls Aloud. He also took on X Factor's Ray Quinn. See www.lbm.ie; phone (020) 7384 0446 or Limerick (061) 340 111.

In Ireland, Mazars O. J. Kilkenny accountants have looked after artists such as U2, Bryan Adams and Chris De Burgh. Call them in Dublin on (01) 449 4400.

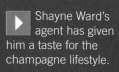
Shayne Ward's agent has given him a taste for the champagne lifestyle.

AGENTS
GET US A GIG!

THE BEST ADVICE I ever got was from an agent who told me: if you want loyalty in the music business, buy a dog. That came from John Giddings who is a giant in the UK music industry. Unfortunately, it's not the job of an agent to dole out sage advice; the agent's job is to book and manage artists' live shows.

Shayne Ward was in a pop band called Destiny for four and a half years, and they had three agents who found them work at the weekends. 'We made about thirty pounds a gig each, which wasn't a lot of money,' he says. 'But when you're paid thirty pounds to do something you love, it feels like Christmas!'

HOW DO AGENTS WORK?

The agent's objective is to find you work: if you don't earn money, neither do they. Larger agents will only take on signed acts. However, there are entertainment agencies or bookers that provide work for unsigned artists in clubs, pubs and on the local circuit.

When I started out I was a booker – a kind of junior agent. Those booking the bigger national or international acts were known as agents; bookers always dealt with smaller acts. These days everyone likes to be called an 'agent'.

If you are lucky enough to find a reputable agent who is willing to put you on the books, you will be expected to sign a contract. This will contain the agreed duration of the contract and details of the commission payable – usually 10 per cent.

Remember: if you're just starting out, arrangements are fairly ad hoc. It's likely that your agent will receive a deposit for each booking, but it's possible you will be expected to collect your fee directly from the client on the night. You are then expected to pay the 10 per cent commission to your agent. A signed artist is unlikely to handle money, as the agent will deal directly with larger venues and bigger promoters on your behalf.

HOW DO I GET AN AGENT?

You need, literally, to have your act together. An agent makes money through taking commission on your earnings. Naturally they are only interested in taking on people who they think have the potential to earn money. If they take on someone who doesn't put on a polished and professional performance, they risk losing business themselves.

They are looking for acts with a polished image and a good demo and press pack to send out to clients. Their artists will be reliable, have their own transport, and experience of performing live. Those who are most successful tend to be those who can perform skilful covers of hit songs. When you can play live for at least two sets of forty-five minutes, you're ready to send your demo and press pack (see D for Demos and P for Press Pack) to an agent.

> *An agent is a person who gets sore because the artist gets ninety per cent of what they make.*
>
> Elton John

FAST TRACK TO FINDING AGENTS

Check out The Agents' Association in the UK and Northern Ireland, which has an online directory of 400 agencies covering every field of light entertainment. Some of the entries list the artists they already represent. See www.agents-uk.com.

Also see the National Entertainment Agents' Council, which is another trade organization for agents. You can see their online database of members at www.neac.org.

The entertainment directory at www.entsweb.co.uk has a list of entertainment agencies, many of whom provide acts for weddings, parties, etc.

Good entertainment agencies in the UK include The Jason West Agency at www.jasonwest.com; phone (01553) 617586, and The Norman Phillips Organization at www.normanphillips.co.uk; phone (01543) 263136.

I also worked for many years with Carol Hanna who runs the largest showbiz agency in Ireland. See www.carolandassociates.com; phone (01) 490 9339. There's also the Irish entertainment agency Audio Networks at www.audionetworks.ie; phone (01) 284 1224. You could also check out the Yellow Pages directory or www.yell.com in the UK, or the Golden Pages directory or www.goldenpages.ie in Ireland.

FAST TRACK TO BEING A DIY AGENT

You can, of course, act as your own agent and send out press packs to clubs, pubs and hotels, or advertise with wedding fairs or other music sites yourself. For more details and tips, see L for Live Performing.

Having an experienced agent is probably beneficial, as he or she is likely to be able to negotiate better fees than you would. This may increase your income, save you time and cover the agent's commission too. Also, some venues fill their entire calendar from a single agent for an all-in annual fee, so they will not be interested in dealing with an individual act.

THE GREAT AGENTS

The following are some of the biggest and best agents in the business.

John Giddings

John Giddings of the Solo Agency is the biggest music agent in Britain, and works with acts such as U2, Celine Dion, Madonna, Phil Collins, David Bowie, Westlife, Rod Stewart and Il Divo. The list of international and UK acts he has worked with is endless.

Solomon Parker

Solomon Parker of The William Morris Agency has taken up where his late father, Louis, left off. He's another great agent to work with. He represents a roster of artists that includes Shayne Ward, Girls Aloud, Take That, All Saints, Jamelia, The Prodigy and Dannii Minogue.

Paul Franklin

Paul Franklin of Helter Skelter in London is another red-hot agent, while Emma Banks in the same company is a great rock agent who works with the likes of the Red Hot Chili Peppers.

FAST TRACK TIP FOR FAME

Take every opportunity to perform live. Even if your ultimate aim is to be an international pop star, don't turn your nose up at corporate work, club gigs, cruise stints or weddings if you're lucky enough to get them. Not only are they a lucrative source of income, they provide artists with valuable experience.

Many people are happy to continue performing at that level, and that's fine. What's wrong with making a living in a business you love? However, if you are focused on pop world domination, then local gigs are a useful stepping stone to greater things.

DON'T CALL US, WE'LL CALL

▶ A baby-faced Colin Farrell posed between Mark Walton (*left*) and Shane Lynch (*right*) at the Boyzone auditions.

HOLLYWOOD HEART-THROB Colin Farrell turned up for the first auditions I ever organized. The auditions on Thursday, 18 November 1993 were for Boyzone. Of course, he wasn't Tinseltown star Colin Farrell back then. He was with the Assets Model Agency in Dublin, and was making a living modelling and demonstrating Texan line dancing around the clubs (it was big at the time).

I thought Colin looked like a star even then. He stood out from the crowd in his bandana, denim jacket and leathers and all the girls flocked around him. He looked so cool for an Irish kid in the early nineties that I decided I wanted him for Boyzone.

I met him one night in the POD nightclub in Dublin and asked him to audition. We only talked for a while, but he seemed to be an eager, nice, well-brought-up kid who wasn't too cocky. He agreed to come to the auditions, although he warned me he couldn't sing.

'My real interest is acting,' he said.
'You've no hope,' I replied. 'You might as well say you're planning to be permanently unemployed.'

The week of the auditions saw Take That mania across Ireland, as the band was performing in Dublin that weekend. Because the notion of setting up a boyband was a real novelty, I managed to get a lot of publicity in the national papers. Yet there was little belief that an Irish act could succeed on the international pop scene. As a result, just thirty-three guys turned up for the Boyzone auditions at The Ormonde Hotel in Dublin.

Among them was Colin. He sang George Michael's 'Careless Whisper' and it was clear that he didn't have a note in his head.

I still might have put him in the band, but I'd already found Ronan Keating and Ronan didn't like Colin. Maybe he saw him as a threat, but he was dead set against him being in the band. I thought the last thing we needed was a potential conflict so I dropped the idea of bringing Colin on board. I think it's fair to say he's done well for himself despite not making the band!

At the end of the night Colin Farrell was out and we had whittled the other guys down to nine pop wannabes. The shortlist for Boyzone was Mark Dalton, Richard Rock,

YOU

Bootilicious Beyonce would storm any audition.

We all of us are stars and we all deserve to twinkle.
Marilyn Monroe

Stephen Gately, Keith Duffy, Shane Lynch, Ronan Keating, Mikey Graham, Karl Power and all-Ireland break dancer, Jason Farrell.

First I decided to drop Mikey Graham, Karl Power and Jason Farrell, and the remaining six made the cut.

Weeks later, Mark Dalton was out and Mikey Graham was in. And just before we were signed by Polydor, we dropped Richard Rock. Richard, the son of a famous Irish showband star called Dickie Rock, just wasn't committed to the band. He stopped believing it might happen when they didn't get signed immediately. He wasn't showing up for gigs and was generally being troublesome. The final straw was when he didn't turn up for a showcase with East 17's manager, Tom Watkins, in the Rock Garden in Dublin.

John Reynolds and I were co-managers of Boyzone at this stage. We didn't know for sure but we were beginning to suspect that Richard was using drugs, which is just a huge, red flashing light for me. I can't stand drugs and it's a definite no-no when you're trying to set up a squeaky-clean boyband aimed at pre-teens and teenagers. His whole attitude was wrong. So, we arranged to meet him and told him he was out of the band. He said 'whatever', or something like that, and sauntered off.

The successful five who emerged from the auditions to form Boyzone.

BOYZONE BEGINNINGS

It turned out our suspicions were right, and he soon had a drug problem that spiralled out of control. His regrets over missing the whole Boyzone thing didn't help and he ended up battling heroin addiction for a long time. Thankfully, he has now come out the other side and has been drug-free for several years.

I really did feel for him. Richard was left with a very bitter pill to swallow as he watched Boyzone go from strength to strength without him. It's a difficult thing for any kid to go through. Still, he's just one of hundreds of thousands of casualties that litter the music industry's Hall of Nearly Famous.

Justin Timberlake in his cocoon stage.

AUDITION HELL

Shayne Ward experienced bitter disappointment when he was dropped from the last thirty on *Popstars: The Rivals* in 2002, but he didn't give up. He kept honing his craft, working at his singing, and he came back again. He showed up at the *X Factor* auditions in 2004 with his group, Destiny. They didn't even make it past the first audition. Then he came back on his own in 2005 and won *X Factor*.

By then he was a completely different person to the one who'd appeared on *Popstars* aged eighteen. It had taken five years of hard work for him to mature into the great artist he is now. (For more details on the *X Factor* auditions, go to X for X Factor.)

I also remember Justin Timberlake when he was with *NSYNC many years ago. With his silly, curly mop of hair, no one gave him a second glance. If anyone had told me that he would become one of the biggest solo stars in the world, I would never have believed them. It took another ten years, but finally a butterfly emerged from the cocoon. The phrase 'A star is born' is not always applicable; sometimes it takes many years for a star to hit his or her stride. 'A star evolves' might be a more appropriate description.

Will Young appeared on *World Idol* in December 2003, competing against other *Pop Idol* winners from around the globe. His performance of 'Light My Fire' was praised by judge Simon Cowell, yet he was blasted by the other judges. Canadian judge, Zack Werner, announced that he hated his performance; Lebanese judge, Elias Rahbani, advised him to get singing lessons. **Even someone as talented as Will Young is not going to please all of the people all of the time.**

It's hard being judged and it's hard being rejected, but it's part of this business and it's certainly part of the audition process. Auditions are basically job interviews for performers. And, like every interview, you will only succeed in getting the job if you are right for it.

FAST TRACK TO SUCCESSFUL AUDITIONS

Look Confident

Introduce yourself and speak clearly and confidently, even if you don't actually feel it. Wear a smile. Look as though you're enjoying yourself and not as though you're in front of a firing squad. An audition is about looking for stars, not timid church mice.

Songs

Select two songs that you love, that you're comfortable with and that show off your voice. Don't go outside your comfort zone. Steer clear of songs by divas such as Aretha Franklin, Mariah Carey, Whitney Houston and Christina Aguilera. Find a song that's a bit unusual or take on a classic song and put your individual stamp on it. I know from personal experience how hard it is to stay awake through countless bad versions of 'I Will Always Love You', 'The Greatest Love of All' and 'Flying Without Wings'.

Get to the Best Part First

Less is definitely more. If the song takes a while to reach the 'good part', skip the start and sing only the chorus. You might have just seconds before they call 'Next!', so make sure those seconds count.

Don't Make Excuses

Don't apologize in advance of your audition. No one wants to hear that they're about to listen to a bad audition because you've got a sore throat, blocked sinuses or you were up all night. We're sick of being told hard-luck stories. Just get on with it. And please, no whining about 'I haven't had a chance to practise', 'Nobody told me' or 'I didn't know'. It's lazy, it's disrespectful and it's very annoying.

Know Your Song

Know the words of the song or songs that you want to perform inside out. No one wants to see that blank stare and goldfish mouth during an audition. Nerves won't wash either. If you can't handle the pressure of a small audition, how do you expect to handle a live audience? The only time you should read lyrics or music is if you are given something specific to perform. Even then, make sure you look up and let the judges see you sing. If possible, find out in advance whether you will be singing with a pianist, a capella, or if it's OK to bring a backing track.

Look Smart and Look the Part

What's wrong with looking like a star? Image is hugely important in the world of show business, yet, incredibly, many turn up for auditions looking like disinterested slobs. If you can't be bothered, how do you expect anyone else to take you seriously? If you want to be a star, make it easy for those auditioning you and look like one. Be warned, this is not an invitation to arrive looking like a complete plonker from a bad rap video. Lose the shades, the bling and the attitude.

Should You Even Be There?

Don't waste people's time. Make sure you fit the criteria for the audition you are attending. Also remember that looks and image can be improved, you can be taught to dance, but the one thing no one can really help you with is a genuine singing voice. It still amazes me how many people come to auditions who haven't a note in their heads. Some people just can't sing. Accept that a career as a singer might not be for you and move on. See V for Vocals for more details on how to improve your singing voice.

Don't Take It Personally

▶ Steer clear of songs by divas like Mariah Carey.

If you are turned down, accept that you are simply not the right person for that particular job at that particular time. It doesn't mean you're not talented or you don't have a future in the music industry. Get over it. Try again and again. You may do fifty auditions and get nowhere because the competition is fierce. Look on every audition as a learning experience that gives you more practice in performing live.

FAST TRACK TO FINDING AUDITIONS

There are hundreds of recruitment agencies, websites and publications that list audition notices. Go straight to J for Jobs for the best of them. Another place to find details of auditions for professional singers and pop star wannabes is the recruitment section of *Stage* magazine. See www.thestage.co.uk.

Also, don't forget to search for singers on the UK Government's Job Centre Plus site on www.jobseekers.direct. It's surprising what you find there sometimes.

Backing Tracks
Bands

POCKET-SIZED BANDS

Mary J. Blige landed her first job (singing backing vocals for such rappers as Father MC) after her stepfather passed a recording – made in a karaoke booth while hanging out at a mall – to a friend at Uptown Records.

Blender magazine

WESTLIFE'S FIRST PROFESSIONAL gig was as the support act for the American chart-toppers the Backstreet Boys, at the RDS in Dublin in 1998. I'd only met the guys a couple of weeks earlier and I still wasn't sure if I was going to manage them.

I heard that promoter Peter Aiken was looking to fill a support slot and I managed to persuade him that Westlife were a fantastic pop act from Sligo. What I didn't tell him was that they were mostly schoolboys who didn't have a set list, didn't have a backing band and didn't have any dance routines.

'Get three songs, get the music on a backing tape and be ready to perform live in a week's time,' I told them. 'You're supporting the Backstreet Boys.'

They picked three songs: 'Together Girl Forever', 'Everlasting Love' and The Who's 'Pinball Wizard'. They got the backing tracks, and after school every day they rehearsed, put together dance routines and styled themselves from a clothes rail in a local shop. One week later they were on stage at the RDS performing as the support act for the Backstreet Boys. They loved every minute of it.

They were able to perform on one of Ireland's largest stages without the expense of musicians or backing singers, thanks to the magic of backing tracks. The self-motivation and drive that they showed that week persuaded me to sign them as my next act.

NO BAND? NO WORRIES

Backing tracks are simply musical recordings from which the vocals are missing. That's where you come in and showcase your talent as a singer or a band. Music purists recoil at the notion of using backing tracks rather than live musicians, but this is the only way most pop acts can afford to perform live. As you gain experience as a performer, you may meet other musicians and decide to form a band. In the meantime, any pop act can put together a slick routine using backing tracks.

When you're ready to perform in public, all you need is a PA (public address) system and, hey presto, you're a one-man or one-woman band!

BACKING MUSIC FOR ORIGINAL SONGS

Singer-songwriters have the option of performing with guitar or piano accompaniment if they play such instruments. If they don't, they can also record original backing tracks to their own songs. Smaller studios with one or two resident musicians or producers can help a singer-songwriter put together an original backing track at a reasonable cost. You may also have friends with the software and know-how to make original music on their computer. Westlife's Mark Feehily is a bit of a music genius with his Apple Mac, and can put together full production backing tracks that sound incredible.

Alternatively, find music producers who are looking for singers. They advertise in music magazines, recording studios or papers such as *Loot* – available at www.loot.com. Many will be happy to trade vocal work for an original backing track. Hiring your own musicians and sessions singers is a costly alternative.

WHICH BACKING TRACKS CAN I USE LIVE?

Backing tracks usually come as MIDI files or karaoke files.

Karaoke backing tracks, which are available on CD in record stores, are handy tools for rehearsal. However, they're not usually licensed for live public performance.

MIDI files are for professional and aspiring musicians; they're usually of better quality and are fully licensed for public performance. The lyrics are often embedded in the MIDI file and can be viewed karaoke-style when played through the correct hardware or software.

FAST TRACK TO GETTING A BACKING TRACK

You can get backing tracks for thousands of hits from a variety of companies on the internet. They are available as instant MP3 downloads for around £6 each, or via mail order on CD for £8. Customers in Ireland will usually have to pay extra for postage and packing. Try www.backtracksonline.co.uk, www.chartmidis.co.uk or www.tune1000.co.uk.

Chappells of Bond Street has a limited selection of backing tracks on CD. Find them at 160 Wardour Street, London; phone (020) 7432 4400.

In Ireland, try Sounds Around, which has a selection of karaoke CDs suitable for starting out. Find them at 9 Capel Street, Dublin 1; phone (01) 873 1029 or see www.soundsaround.ie.

TEAM PLAYER OR SOLO DIVA?

> *I had a dream and it was fulfilled by meeting Benny, Björn and Agnetha.*
>
> Anni-Frid Lyngstad of ABBA

LIFE IS CERTAINLY less complicated for the solo diva, who has complete artistic and financial control over his or her career. The likes of Ronan Keating, Shayne Ward, Madonna, Justin Timberlake, Britney Spears and Christina Aguilera don't need to consult anyone else when they want to make a decision concerning their career. You should remember, however, that Ronan Keating and Justin Timberlake were previously members of the boybands Boyzone and *NSYNC respectively, while Britney and Christina may not have come from girl bands, but they were two of many Disney Mouseketeers!

Justin Timberlake started out as a team player with *NSYNC and ended up a solo diva.

In fact you'll find most of the big music stars have used previous careers in bands as their springboard for solo success. Lionel Richie was a Commodore; George Michael started out in Wham!; Robbie Williams was a member of Take That; Michael Jackson was one of the Jackson Five; Donny Osmond performed with the Osmonds; Paul McCartney was a Beatle; bootilicious Beyoncé was with Destiny's Child . . . do I need to go on? And record companies are more likely to sign artists who already have a devoted following.

SOLO OR BAND ROUTE?

Sure, a singer can always choose to go it alone. As discussed, singer-songwriters can perform live with guitar or piano, while pop singers can perform solo with the help of backing tracks and a PA system. At the same time, starting out can be more fun if you're surrounded and supported by peers who share your dreams and ambitions.

Yet there can be major drawbacks to being in a band. Every group starts out well, but it's no fun when members start to get on each other's nerves. So think carefully before you decide to join or set up a band. There are a lot of things to take into consideration before you invest time, money and ambition in another bunch of people.

THE BAND AGREEMENT

So it's decided. You are to become part of a group. Great! Let's ensure that it doesn't all end in tears by setting up a band agreement (these are also called partnership agreements, because bands are partnerships in the eyes of the law).

The band agreement should detail what happens to the name of the band in the event of a split. You must decide who 'owns' the name. If a band is signed, this is out of your hands, as the record company usually holds the right to decide who keeps the name.

There may be other assets, such as musical instruments or a van. If these were bought as a group, their division must also be noted in the band agreement. Details of how the band's income is split should also be included. See C for Copyright on how the revenue from your songs can be shared.

There are lots of issues to be dealt with in a band agreement, but it could save a great deal of time and trouble in the long run if things turn sour.

FAST TRACK TO A BAND AGREEMENT

The Musicians' Union – www.musiciansunion.org.uk – can provide you with a partnership fact file, a sample partnership agreement and even free legal advice on a band agreement. See U for Unions for details on how to join.

THINGS TO CONSIDER

★ Are you all living in the same area so that you can rehearse and meet easily?
★ Do the rest of the band have the same ambition for world chart domination as you do?
★ Are they truly committed or are they just doing this for a laugh at weekends?
★ Does everyone want to make the same music, and are they capable of doing so?
★ How competent are your bandmates vocally and at playing instruments?
★ Are they as reliable and dedicated as you are to following your dream?

The band broke up because I couldn't bear (Johnny) Rotten any more because he was an embarrassment with his silly hats and his, like, shabby, dirty, nasty-looking appearance.

Sid Vicious of the Sex Pistols

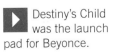

Destiny's Child was the launch pad for Beyonce.

THE BIG QUESTION

Are you a team player who is willing to put the interests of the group first, rather than your own? If not, step away from the band! Problems usually start when one member gets more attention than the rest.

The fact is that there is only one frontman or woman in every band. In U2 it's Bono. In the Rolling Stones it's Mick Jagger. In Boyzone it was Ronan Keating. In Westlife it's Shane Filan. In the Pussycat Dolls it's Nicole Scherzinger.

Are you prepared to make someone else look good if you're not that frontman or woman? If not, maybe joining a band is not a good idea.

FAST TRACK TO FINDING A BAND

Student noticeboards are a good place to start. Larry Mullen of U2 pinned a note to the one at his school and it worked out well for him. You can also meet like-minded people in local music shops and independent record stores. Rehearsal studios usually have noticeboards where you and other wandering music souls can advertise for bandmates.

Also check out www.musicianseeksmusician.com. Rock artists advertise in *NME* magazine in the UK or *Hot Press* magazine in Ireland. The Irish site www.CPU.ie also has a musician's forum. If you're looking to set up a pop band you should watch or advertise in *Stage* magazine in the UK, or at local stage schools. Local freesheets and papers such as *Loot* – available at www.loot.com – are also good places to look.

LOUIS'S ALL-TIME DREAM BOYBAND

Shane Filan (Westlife): Lead vocalist
Brian Littrell (Backstreet Boys): Second lead vocalist
Gary Barlow (Take That): Songwriter
Justin Timberlake (*NSYNC): Band heart-throb
Ronan Keating (Boyzone): Band golden boy

LOUIS'S ALL-TIME DREAM GIRL BAND

Beyoncé (Destiny's Child): Sex bomb lead vocalist
Nicole Scherzinger (Pussycat Dolls): Spare sex-bomb lead vocalist
Heidi Range (Sugababes): The obligatory blonde
Jodi Albert (Girl Thing): Sweetheart appeal with incredible voice
Nadine Coyle (Girls Aloud): Leggy Irish songbird

Charts
Choreography
Collection Societies
Concerts
Copyright

IT'S THE FINAL COUNTDOWN

Boyzone worked hard for their first Number 1 and then the hits avalanched.

> *In the past, record companies were committed to working a band over several singles — not just giving up if the first single didn't set the charts on fire.*
>
> Graham Nash of Crosby, Stills, Nash & Young

I CAN'T WAIT for the charts to come out on a Sunday. So instead I get the mid-week charts on a Tuesday morning. It doesn't matter whether any of my acts have a single out or not, I still love to know what's going on. The mid-week charts are the first sales indications and are made available to record companies; they're usually a fairly accurate indication of the way the Top 20 will look on Sunday.

Music legend Elton John is the same. **Elton is a big music fan. He loves going into record stores and buying up armfuls of the latest CDs.** He loves listening to all the latest artists and he really loves the charts. He told me he always makes a call to his record company on a Tuesday morning to find out what the latest charts are like.

My biggest chart thrill was the release of Boyzone's first UK single, 'Love Me For A Reason', in 1995. The single had been released by Polydor in Ireland and went to Number 1. Yet most people in the UK record company didn't want to know about Boyzone. They regarded the label in Ireland as little more than a warehouse for shipping their products and they didn't rate the boys. We knew that if the UK didn't release the single, the band was as good as finished.

The key to Boyzone's success was getting the band on the *Smash Hits* Roadshow, during which they performed at a series of pop shows around the UK. The guys worked their magic, charming fans and organizers alike. The roadshow culminated in a grand finale called the *Smash Hits* Poll Winners' Party, broadcast live on TV in the UK. Boyzone won a gong for 'Best Band on the Road' and collected their award before

25,000 hysterical pop fans and 11 million viewers. Then they got the cover of *Smash Hits* magazine. Polydor in the UK couldn't ignore Boyzone any longer.

They released the single in December 1995. We had no idea how it was going to do but we prayed and promoted desperately for the Top 20. I'll never forget receiving the mid-week charts that Tuesday morning and discovering they were Number 2. East 17's huge hit 'Stay Another Day' kept us from going to Number 1, but it didn't matter because being in the Top 5 with our first single was

beyond any of our wildest dreams. 'Love Me For A Reason' went on to sell over 700,000 copies and made the Top 10 in most European countries. It's what made the record company think, 'hang on, we may be on to something here', and finally throw their weight behind us.

Me and Sharon Osbourne with Elton John and partner, David Furnish.

My second biggest chart thrill was the Boyzone single 'Words' giving the boys their first UK Number 1 in October 1996. After that, everything just avalanched and we had a total of six Number 1 singles, sixteen Top 3 singles, twenty appearances on *Top of the Pops* and four Number 1 albums. Chart bliss!

FAST TRACK TO THE CHARTS

Who Compiles the Charts?

The official UK charts are compiled by The Official UK Charts Company for the BPI (British Phonographic Industry) and ERA (Entertainment Retailers Association). The Irish charts are compiled by Chart Track for IRMA (Irish Recorded Music Association).

How Are the Charts Compiled?

The charts are compiled using a computer system that can read sales data from record stores and internet retailers across the UK and Ireland. In the UK over 5,800 outlets, including all the big high street chains, 600 independent stores and all major internet retailers are linked to a central computer that reads the barcode of every item as it is sold. The information is collected from Sunday through to Saturday, and the official chart is revealed at 4 p.m. every Sunday on BBC Radio 1.

In Ireland the charts are compiled from CD sales in 400 stores around the country, along with the download sales from top internet retailers. The data is collected from Friday to Thursday evening the following week, and the Irish charts are announced on RTE 2FM on Fridays at 6 p.m.

How Many Records Are Sold Each Week?

An average of 1 million singles and 3 million albums are sold each week.

How Many Sales Do You Need for a Number 1 Single?

The Official UK Charts Company says that Number 1 records have sold an average of 133,000 copies per week over the last decade. However, I know plenty of Number 1 hits with sales of 50,000 singles. Sales of 25,000 or so will usually guarantee a Top 10 hit, and the easiest month to get into the Top 10 is early January when sales are lower. In Ireland you need to shift a few thousand for a Number 1 hit.

What's the Best Way of Getting a Number 1?

The best way of boosting sales and getting a Number 1 is the old-fashioned way: personal appearances in record stores. There's nothing like a record signing in stores around the country to ensure big sales. It's hard work, but I've done it with acts lots of times in the UK and Ireland, and it rarely fails.

How Do You Get a Gold, Silver or Platinum Record?

The sales needed for a gold, silver or platinum record differ in every country, depending on the population of each region. The UK has different certification quantities for singles and albums. Ireland and America's certification systems are similar, except for the vast differences in sales required. The American music industry also has a unique and much coveted diamond record for sales of over 10 million units!

	SILVER	GOLD	PLATINUM	DIAMOND
UK SINGLES	200,000	400,000	600,000	n/a
UK ALBUMS	60,000	100,000	300,000	n/a
IRISH SINGLES & ALBUMS	n/a	7,500	15,000	n/a
US SINGLES & ALBUMS	n/a	500,000	1 million	10 million

Where Do You Find the UK and Irish Charts?

The UK charts are available at www.theofficialcharts.com, and can be heard on *Radio 1's Chart Show* every Sunday and through the Radio 1 website. The charts are also published in newspapers and magazines such as *Music Week* and *Billboard*.

The Irish charts are available at www.irma.ie. They can also be heard on RTE 2FM on Fridays at 6 p.m., and are published in some national newspapers such as the *Irish Daily Star*.

LOUIS WALSH'S NUMBER 1 UK HITS

1. Johnny Logan, 'What's Another Year' (17/5/1980)
2. Boyzone, 'Words' (19/10/1996)
3. Boyzone, 'A Different Beat' (14/12/1996)
4. Boyzone, 'All That I Need' (2/5/1998)
5. Boyzone, 'No Matter What' (15/8/1998)
6. Boyzone, 'When The Going Gets Tough' (13/3/1999)
7. Westlife, 'Swear It Again' (1/5/1999)
8. Boyzone, 'You Needed Me' (22/5/1999)
9. Ronan Keating, 'When You Say Nothing At All' (7/8/1999)
10. Westlife, 'If I Let You Go' (21/8/1999)
11. Westlife, 'Flying Without Wings' (30/10/1999)
12. Westlife, 'I Have A Dream'/'Seasons In The Sun' (25/12/1999)
13. Westlife, 'Fool Again' (8/4/2000)
14. Ronan Keating, 'Life Is A Rollercoaster' (22/7/2000)
15. Westlife and Mariah Carey, 'Against All Odds' (30/9/2000)
16. Westlife, 'My Love' (11/11/2000)
17. Westlife, 'Uptown Girl' (17/3/2001)
18. Westlife, 'Queen Of My Heart' (17/11/2001)
19. Westlife, 'World Of Our Own' (2/3/2002)
20. Ronan Keating, 'If Tomorrow Never Comes' (18/5/2002)
21. Westlife, 'Unbreakable' (16/11/2002)
22. Girls Aloud, 'Sound of The Underground' (28/12/2002)
23. Westlife, 'Mandy' (29/11/2003)
24. Girls Aloud, 'I'll Stand By You' (27/11/2004)
25. Westlife, 'You Raise Me Up' (12/11/2005)
26. Shayne Ward, 'That's My Goal' (31/12/2005)
27. Westlife, 'The Rose' (18/11/2006)
28. Girls Aloud vs Sugababes, 'Walk This Way' (23/3/2007)

CHOREOGRAPHY
DANCE TO THE MUSIC

I was always a singer and a dancer and I always wanted to be an actress. For me, it's all just one thing.

Jennifer Lopez

J-Lo started her career as a dancer.

BOYZONE WERE THE most uncoordinated bunch you could meet – they were dunces in the dance department.

'We were brutal dancers,' says Keith Duffy. 'Choreographers just walked out on us. They broke down in tears and walked.

They couldn't take it. Shaun Fernandez ended up as our choreographer because he was the only one who could take it. We couldn't do much so he had to work hard to make us look good doing very little. I was really hardcore bad. I was forever turning the wrong way or doing the wrong thing. We had these little steps during one tour and we were meant to jump up and down off them. Of course, one night I jumped up and my foot went through it and of course, when I tried to pull my foot out it was completely stuck. The lads stopped and p***ed themselves laughing. Then everyone else started laughing. It was a small venue but it's still not very nice to have seventeen hundred people laughing at you. In the end the mistakes became part of our routine. The fans used to tell me that they expected it from me. They told me it was all part of the fun to see how many times Keith would cock up the dance routines.'

> *The one thing that can solve most of our problems is dancing.*
>
> James Brown

As you can see, **the ability to dance is not an absolute necessity for an aspiring pop star, but it's certainly an asset.** It can enhance your stage performance, coordination and posture, and will give you the confidence to move to your own music.

Shayne Ward and Westlife's choreographer is the great Priscilla Samuels, who had worked with the Spice Girls, S Club 7 and Tina Turner before turning her attention to my acts.

'New artists are always full of "scaredness", as I call it,' she laughs. 'Shayne Ward looked like a rabbit caught in the headlights when I asked him to do a step. He had this face like, "you can't be serious. You can't ask me to do that!" '

The Spice Girls learned a few hot moves from choreographer Priscilla Samuels.

She faced the same problems with Westlife, who were complete dance amateurs when she started with them. 'Shane Filan was always a bit quicker picking up the steps because he had a bit of previous dance training,' she said. 'But once the others got over the "scaredness" bit too they were fine. Now I only have to spend ten days in training with them before a tour and they have the routine down.'

Professional dancers make it look easy, but don't be fooled, because the really good ones are true athletes. Learning to dance involves a lot of hard work, sore feet and aching legs. Priscilla insists it's a lot of fun too, and a great way for any artist to get fit.

'I worked with Westlife for eight hours a day this week, but if there are still tears at the end of the day, we'd go another few hours,' she said. 'When the crying stops and they have the moves, we call it a day. It's punishing and they moaned they weren't able to move with the pain after day three last week but we keep going until they've got it.'

Even a solo singer has to work with other dancers on stage or on video. Jennifer Lopez is a film, fashion and music superstar now, but it wasn't so long ago that she made her living as a backing dancer. Her dance skills came to the fore in her music videos.

FINDING YOUR FEET

These days, choreographers use a variety of styles of dance, so ideally you should learn several different dance forms. Yet choreographer Priscilla Samuels rubbishes the notion that you have to attend full-time dance school to become a good dancer. She attended classes three times a week after school while completing her general education. She clearly had a natural ability and quickly developed a passion for dancing. 'Any time there was any call for freestyle dance, I was off,' she said. 'I loved making up dance moves and people said I should do choreography. I got my break working with the artist Cathy Dennis and I've been working for record companies ever since.'

However, you don't need to be planning a career in dance to attend classes; you can go along simply to improve your moves. Alternatively, students aged from eleven to sixteen can attend full-time courses at specialist theatre schools in the UK, which combine dance training and general education. There are also dozens of dance colleges and hundreds of university courses in dance for those interested in full-time study after school. See Q for Qualifications for more details on full-time training.

FAST TRACK TO FINDING DANCE SCHOOLS AND CLASSES

The Council for Dance Education and Training has an online database of teachers and schools offering mostly full-time courses. See www.cdet.org.uk; phone (020) 7247 4030.

The British Dance Council deals with disco freestyle dance, Latin American and ballroom. Contact them at secretary@british-dance-council.org to be emailed a list of dance schools in your area. They will also post you a list if you send a large SAE to The British Dance Council, 240 Merton Road, South Wimbledon, London, SW19 1EQ. Their website is www.british-dance-council.org.

Try the Dance Schools UK and Ireland website www.danceschools-uk.co.uk. Click on the map to find a dance school in your area.

The Dance Theatre of Ireland runs dance classes at its school in Dun Laoghaire, County Dublin. It also runs educational outreach programmes and dance workshops for any group of ten or more. See www.dancetheatreireland.com; phone (01) 280 3455.

Click on the links section on the website of the Association of Professional Dancers in Ireland for details of some dance schools in Ireland. See www.prodanceireland.com.

Try the business telephone directory www.yell.com for local classes in the UK, or www.goldenpages.ie in Ireland.

COLLECTION SOCIETIES
THE DEBT COLLECTORS

[*I'm tired of telling people what they're too lazy to know.*]

Van Morrison

MANY MUSICIANS NEVER make an effort to understand copyright, royalties and collection societies because they see the whole area as a bewildering maze best left to the accountants. However, it's not quite as technical as the music industry sometimes makes out. You just need to understand three things: who each collection agency represents, why they are entitled to payment, and how they go about collecting their payment.

Understanding what the various debt collectors do is the key to unlocking the whole concept of royalties and how to make money in music. And if you're planning a career in the music industry, you'd better find out how you make your money.

Most countries outside the UK and Ireland have their equivalent debt-collecting organizations. They collect the royalties generated by the music of UK and Irish artists in their countries and send them to the agencies here, and vice versa. And, of course, all the agencies make their money by keeping a small percentage of the total amount they collect.

The collection societies ensure 50 Cent doesn't have to Die Tryin' to Get Rich from his albums and movies.

MCPS (MECHANICAL COPYRIGHT PROTECTION SOCIETY – UK AND IRELAND)

WHO? They represent and collect money on behalf of publishers and songwriters.

WHY? Every time music is 'copied' or 'recorded', songwriters and their publishers are entitled to royalty payments known as 'mechanicals'.

WHO PAYS? Record companies must pay mechanical royalties every time they press and sell a copy of a CD. Mechanical royalties also apply when music is used in films or adverts; these are known as synchronization rights. Mechanical royalties are also charged on ringtones, which are now a big earner for songwriters.

HOW? Mechanical royalties of 8.5 per cent are levied on the wholesale price of a record, known as the PPD (Published Price to Dealer).

HOW MUCH TO JOIN?	Songwriters must pay a one-off payment of £50 to join the MCPS in the UK and €80 to join in Ireland.
CONTACT:	MCPS in the UK on **(020) 7560 5544** or **www.mcps-prs-alliance.co.uk**; or in Ireland on **(01) 676 6940** or **www.mcps.ie**.

PRS (PERFORMING RIGHT SOCIETY, UK) / IMRO (IRISH MUSIC RIGHTS ORGANIZATION, IRELAND)

WHO?	This agency represents and collects money on behalf of publishers and songwriters.
WHY?	Every time music – live or recorded – is performed in public, the songwriters and their publishers are entitled to a royalty payment.
WHO PAYS?	Radio and TV broadcasters, venues that host live music concerts, nightclubs, pubs, restaurants, shops – any public place that plays or hosts live or recorded music.
HOW?	Anyone wishing to use copyright music in public must buy a licence. There are blanket licence fees and different tariffs. For instance, hairdressers with up to thirty stylists' chairs will pay £61.89 a year; a factory operating 330 days a year, with seventy employees, playing music seven and a half hours a day, will pay just over £1,000.

Similarly, when music is played live, royalties of 3.25 per cent must be paid to the songwriter. The tariff is based on ticket sales. So say 10,000 fans pay £25 each on the door; the ticket sales amount to £250,000. Multiply £250,000 by 3.25 per cent, which makes a total fee of £8,125. Pubs are charged according to the size of the premises and whether the music comes from a jukebox or from live music. Radio stations pay a percentage of their advertising revenue. The BBC pays according to audience size.

The PRS also calculates who gets paid what through market research. They get playlists from major radio stations and set lists from big live bands. They also sample airplay on radio stations; the only radio station in the UK that is 100 per cent checked is Radio 1.

HOW MUCH TO JOIN?	It costs songwriters £100 to join the PRS. Membership of IMRO is free.
CONTACT:	PRS on **(020) 7580 5544** or **www.mcps-prs-alliance.co.uk**; IMRO on **(01) 661 4844** or see **www.imro.ie**.

PPL (PHONOGRAPHIC PERFORMANCE LIMITED, UK) / PPI (PHONOGRAPHIC PERFORMANCE IRELAND)

WHO? This agency collects money on behalf of record companies and performers. Former performers' associations PAMRA (Performing Artists' Media Rights Association) and AURA (Association of United Recording Artists) are now merged with the PPL.

WHY? Every time a sound recording (usually on a CD, tape or music video) is used in public, record companies and performers (both singers and musicians) are entitled to a royalty payment. In reality, most session singers and musicians consent to waive their royalties for a one-off fee.

WHO PAYS? Radio and TV stations, clubs, shops, pubs, restaurants, bars, hairdressers, waiting rooms, nightclubs – anyone playing recorded music in public, whether it's via radio, TV or CD. Family events such as wedding receptions or birthday parties are exempt; public events such as discos, dinner dances or office parties are not.

HOW? The PPL and PPI issue licences to anyone who wants to play sound recordings in public. There are many different tariffs; you will be told the fee over the telephone. The PPL passes on a share of this income to performers: featured artists, session musicians, orchestral players or singers. In Ireland, the record companies' and performers' income is collected by PPI, but the performers' share is distributed by RAAP (Recording Artists and Performers).

HOW MUCH TO JOIN? No yearly membership for PPL, PPI or RAAP.

CONTACT: PPL in the UK on **(020) 7534 1000** or **www.ppluk.com**; PPI in Ireland on **(01) 280 5977** or **www.ppiltd.com**. RAAP on **(01) 293 4999** or **www.raap.ie**.

[CONCERTS]
WHO ROBBED THE TAKINGS?

YOU'VE HIT THE big time and you've sold out a night at Wembley Arena. A total of 12,000 fans have shelled out a whopping £30 each for a ticket to hear you perform. Do I see pound signs in your eyes? Yes, a total of £360,000 may have been made at the box office in one single night, but don't go booking the suite next door to Simon Cowell in the Sandy Lane Hotel, Barbados just yet.

Huge ticket sales do not always equal huge profits. In fact, touring is often a loss-making promotional device when artists are starting out. And even when you hit the big time, the costs of staging a spectacular concert quickly eat into seven-figure guarantees from the promoter. Let's borrow the accountant's calculator and see exactly where the takings go.

On stage, I'm the happiest person in the world.

Britney Spears

WEMBLEY ARENA GROSS EARNINGS £360,000

(12,000 fans paying £30 per ticket)

PROMOTER'S EXPENSES FOR WEMBLEY ARENA	
Deduct 17.5 per cent VAT in UK (21 per cent in Ireland)	£53,617
Deduct 3 per cent PRS (See C for Collection Societies)	£8,923
Wembley Arena venue hire	£40,000
Riggers to set up stage	£8,000
Staff and security costs	£15,000
Catering	£5,000
Advertising	£40,000
(A one-page advert in the Evening Standard *costs £18,000 alone; three ads per day on Capital Radio costs £12,500 per day)*	
Insurance	£1,000
Cancellation insurance	£2,500
Medical assistance	£2,500
Misc. (phones, towels, extras on rider, taxis, gratuities)	£3,640
Total costs for the promoter (approx.)	**£180,000**
BALANCE AFTER COSTS	£180,000
PROMOTER'S 20 PER CENT SHARE	£36,000
ARTIST'S 80 PER CENT SHARE	£144,000
ARTIST'S EXPENSES ON £144,000 FOR A 30 DATE TOUR	
Minus agent's commission of 10 per cent	£14,000
REHEARSALS	
Studio, hotels, crew food, transport Total: £60,000	
divided by 30 nights. Rehearsal cost per concert:	£2,000
WAGES	
Band, crew, dancers (40 people)	
Total cost: £320,000 divided by 30 nights. Wages cost per concert:	£8,000
PER DIEMS	
Band, crew, dancers (40 people)	
Food allowance @ £30 each per day:	£1,200
STAGE SET	
Design, set, trap doors, lifts, drapes, etc.	
Total cost: £300,000 divided by 30 nights. Stage set cost per night:	£10,000
SHOW PRODUCTION	
Consultant and choreography	
Total: £30,000 divided by 30 nights. Average cost per night:	£1,000

SOUND

PA system, including crew

Total: £110,000 divided by 30 nights. Average cost per night: £3,600

LIGHTING

Lighting, lighting crew, pyrotechnics

Total: £150,000 divided by 30 nights. Average cost per night: £5,000

MUSIC/INSTRUMENTATION

Programming, recording, equipment hire, voiceovers, samplers

Total: £30,000 divided by 30 nights. Average cost per night: £1,000

TRANSPORT

Articulated trucks 8

Total: £100,000 divided by 30 nights. Average cost per night: £3,300

Van hire, production car, fuel, flights, buses

Total: £75,000 divided by 30 nights. Average cost per night: £2,500

ACCOMMODATION

40 hotel rooms @ £125 per night £5,000

WARDROBE

Stylist, band clothes, dancers' wardrobe, musicians' wardrobe,
laundry, storage of wardrobe cases

Total: £100,000 divided by 30 nights. Average cost per night: £3,300

MISC.

Mobile phones, telephones, laminates, itineraries, stationery

Total: £5,000 divided by 30 nights. Average per night: £166

Total costs for the artist £60,066

BALANCE AFTER COSTS **£83,934**

Less management commission of 20 per cent

*(The manager's commission is usually deducted from the
net rather than the gross takings for live performances.)* **£16,786**

NET EARNINGS FOR NIGHT AT WEMBLEY £67,148

Divided by four (in Westlife's case) £16,787 each

Less income tax (40 per cent in UK) £6,714

MONEY IN ARTIST'S POCKET **£10,073**

▶ Razorlight also count the cost to stage a concert at Wembley.

FAST TRACK NOTE

Earning £10,000 for a single night's performance is not to be sniffed at, but remember that this is calculated on a sell-out show of a 12,000-seater venue. The pickings are not as rich in your average 8,000-seater arena, and not many artists will be able to spread the costs over a sell-out thirty-night tour.

FAST TRACK TO THE PROMOTER'S GUARANTEE

Established stars will usually be offered a guaranteed fee to perform; so it doesn't matter if no one turns up, the artist still gets paid. Of course, the artist wouldn't get that guaranteed fee if it wasn't already a given that fans will be clamouring for tickets. The fee is based on a percentage of the concert's income after expenses – anything between 75 per cent and 90 per cent – and will be paid to the artist long before he or she steps on the stage. However, if the show is a complete sell-out and the percentage of income deal works out greater than the guaranteed fee, then the artist receives the balance after the show.

FAST TRACK TO MORE GOOD NEWS

A successful tour not only brings in money from ticket sales, but it also guarantees that record sales will go up, along with the accompanying royalties. And your publishing royalties will also increase if you perform your own music. In fact, you will get back much of the £8,923 fee you paid to the PRS for your Wembley Arena concert (see above). And of course, merchandising sales will soar, which can amount to £7 per T-shirt in your pocket! (See M for Merchandise.)

COPYRIGHT
THE RIGHT TO MAKE MONEY

Robbie Williams got into a legal wrangle over his hit, Angels.

THERE'S AN OLD saying in the music business: Where there's a hit, there's a writ. Many top artists, including Robbie Williams, Britney Spears and Madonna, have been sued by songwriters for copyright infringement.

Singer Robbie Williams got into a legal wrangle with Irish singer-songwriter Ray Heffernan over the monster hit 'Angels'. The pair co-wrote a song over Christmas 1996 which they called 'An Angel Instead'. Ray got in touch with the record company when he heard that his song was going to be on Robbie's album. He was offered £7,500 for his share. He was twenty-three, broke and naive, so he took it. 'Angels' went on to become a worldwide hit and Ray called in the legal eagles, but there was nothing he could do; he had already sold his copyright. The lucrative spoils for 'Angels' are now shared between the copyright owners, Robbie Williams and his former songwriting partner, Guy Chambers.

Madonna was also in the wars with a songwriter in Belgium who claimed that her 1998 hit 'Frozen' was a copy of one of his songs. The judge agreed that the record company and Madonna had used four bars of the French-language song.

WHAT IS COPYRIGHT?

The actual term 'copyright' refers to a whole number of rights that come into play when a songwriter creates music, a singer sings this music, and a record company records it. Copyright protects everyone in the music business, and ensures that all those who had a hand in the creation of the music are rewarded. Songwriters, singers, publishers and record companies are able to make a living from their creative efforts thanks to copyright. For more details on how you make money through copyright, see R for Royalties.

TYPES OF COPYRIGHT

Songwriters' Copyright

If you write a song, you automatically own the copyright of the words and music. However, you need to protect that copyright by establishing when the song was created in case someone else tries to claim they wrote it first (see 'Fast Track to Protecting Copyright' on page 54). Every time that song is performed publicly, on the radio, in a supermarket or on stage, royalties have to be paid.

The songwriter also holds the mechanical copyright, which relates to CD recordings of the song. Every time that song is pressed and sold on CD, the writer receives royalties.

Recording Copyright

Recording copyright is owned by the company who made the recording – usually the record company. They pay for the recording and then recoup their money via sales and royalties. The record companies make money every time a record is sold. They also receive royalties every time their recordings are broadcast or performed publicly, whether in a restaurant, a nightclub or on a radio station.

The record companies are represented by the PPL (Phonographic Performance Ltd) in the UK and the PPI (Phonographic Performance Ireland) in Ireland (see C for Collection Societies).

Performers' Copyright

All artists and performers, featured and non-featured, are entitled to a payment when a sound recording that they have contributed to is broadcast publicly.

A session singer who was paid £30 to perform on Pink Floyd's *Dark Side of the Moon* in 1973 won an out-of-court settlement from the record label and the band in 2005. The court sided with Clare Torry when she claimed that she deserved half-ownership of the copyright as she used a special 'wailing' technique on the recording; her contribution was deemed distinctive enough to deserve royalties. No one knows how much she got in the settlement, but as the album sold 36 million copies and was in the charts for twenty-six years, we can assume it was substantial!

However, session musicians and singers usually sign a waiver to royalties in return for a one-off fee.

Royalties are collected by the PPL (Phonographic Performance Limited) in the UK and the PPI (Phonographic Performance Ireland) in Ireland (see C for Collection Societies).

HOW LONG DOES COPYRIGHT LAST?

Songwriters own copyright of their songs for the duration of their lives and seventy years after their death, so even your great-grandchildren may enjoy the fruits of your labour.

Performers only own copyright of their performances for fifty years. The music industry in the UK and Ireland has been waging a battle to increase this current fifty-year limit to the same ninety-five years that is enjoyed in the United States.

Warring Oasis brothers, Noel and Liam, don't share songwriting credits.

Cliff Richard is one of the first big stars to be affected by this, as his copyright on the 1959 hit 'Living Doll' runs out in 2009. Many stars of the fifties have already lost out on their performance royalties at a time when they are retired and could do with a boost to their pensions.

FAST TRACK TO SHARING COPYRIGHT

So what happens to the copyright if you co-write a song? There are no set rules on how to split the copyright. If there are two of you and you both contribute equally to the song, it's easy to suggest splitting the songwriting royalties fifty-fifty. And if one person only makes a minimal contribution, it's possible to agree to a 5 per cent songwriting credit.

However, copyright can be a big bone of contention as it is one of the major sources of income in music. Some of the world's most successful bands have decided to overcome this problem by sharing copyright equally: **U2, REM and Coldplay all split their songwriting income evenly between band members.** Oasis, on the other hand, don't share songwriting credits. I don't know if this is the source of a lot of their well-publicized bickering, but it could be a contributing factor!

FAST TRACK TO PROTECTING COPYRIGHT

American songwriters can register songs with the Copyright Office of the United States, but there is no such formal registration of songs in the UK and Ireland.

As soon as you write or record a song, copyright is automatically created. You still need to prove when you created that work to ensure no one else claims it as their song at a later date. To do this, you post a recording of the song or a copy of the sheet music to yourself by registered post; it's also recommended that you enclose the front page of a newspaper in the envelope. Write the song title on the envelope before you post it. Keep the envelope sealed and the postage receipt in a safe place and hope that you will never have to open it in a court room.

You should also keep a record of who you have sent the song to – record companies, publishers or artists. Don't rely on your memory.

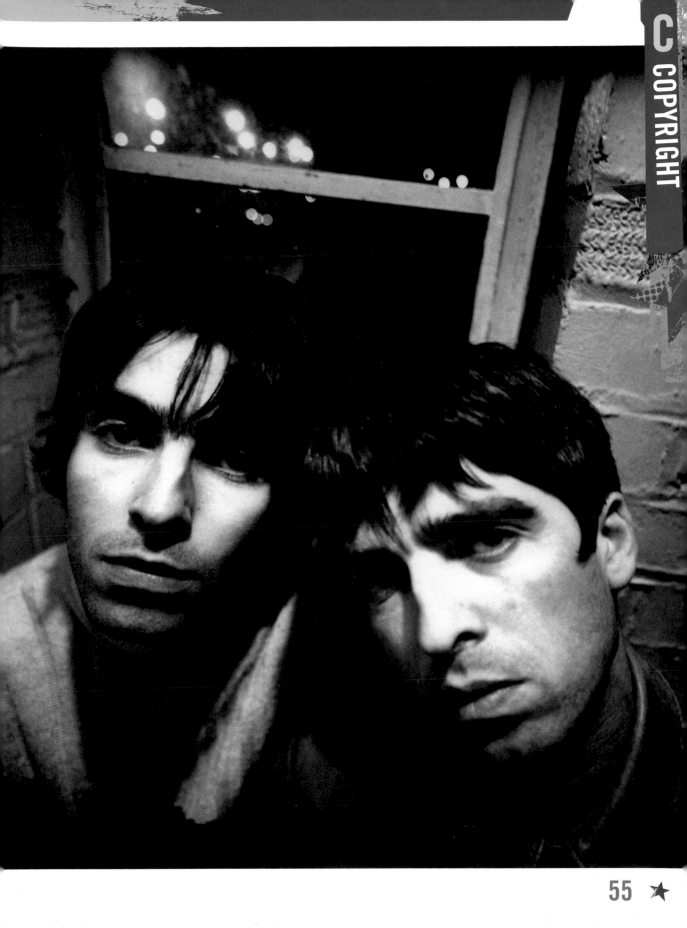

D

DIY
Demos
Directories

DIY

GOING IT ALONE

ESSEX ROCK BAND Koopa made history as the first unsigned act to enter the UK Top 40 in January 2007; singer-songwriter David Gray beat the business when he recorded the album *White Ladder* in his bedroom and sold 6 million units; **Damien Rice also recorded his million-selling début album, *O*, in the comfort of his bedroom in County Kildare in Ireland.**

David Gray and Damien Rice – from recording in their bedrooms, to Live Earth at Wembley Stadium in July 2007.

Another Irish singer-songwriter, Julie Feeney, self-financed and released her own début album, *13 Songs*. She only released the album in Ireland, but she still managed to get it reviewed by the *New York Times*, which described it as 'a charming, urbane, dreamy record'. Little surprise then that she landed a worldwide deal with Sony late in 2006.

HOW ARE SO MANY ARTISTS ABLE TO GO IT ALONE THESE DAYS?

It's all thanks to the combination of the internet and new affordable recording technology. Emerging artists no longer have to be signed to a label to create and market their material and so make a living in the business. They can record cheaply thanks to inexpensive technology and distribute it via the internet. In fact, artists who put out their own records will actually make a lot more money per album than if they released it through a record company.

It's still hard to match record companies in terms of the volume of sales they are able to achieve, yet even established artists such as Mick Hucknall and Chris de Burgh are now releasing downloads or CDs of new material via their websites.

FAST TRACK TIP

The internet is a vital and cost-effective tool for any artist going it alone. See I for Internet for more DIY details and how to become 'virtually' famous.

RECORDING STUDIOS

Time is money in the recording studio, and when you arc releasing your own record, time is *your* money. Don't use the studio for rehearsals; make sure you're fully prepared and ready to lay down those tracks. There are huge differences in recording studio costs. Local studios charge around £200 per day in the UK, while bigger ones charge far more. Prices in Ireland vary considerably too, but, as a guide, Asylum Studios on Dublin's Abbey Street charges €350 per day.

Ask other artists to recommend studios – especially ones with good in-house engineers, musicians and technicians – and talk to people in local music shops or record stores. You'll find listings of recording studios on the business directory site **www.yell.com** in the UK, or **www.goldenpages.ie** in Ireland. Or see D for Directories.

HOME RECORDING STUDIOS

An inexperienced act will probably need the help of a producer and the facilities of a professional studio to make the most of their sound. Having said that, if you fancy yourself as a bit of a studio whiz, off you go.

Once upon a time, music nerds spent a fortune on multi-track recorders, miles of cable, outboard gear processors and piles of expensive hardware. Today, the biggest outlay for a home studio will be a computer or a digital multi-tracker. And most people already have a computer, so that's half the battle. Setting up a modern, home recording studio and your own record label is now more about buying software than bulky hardware.

The best way to set up your own studio is to link up with another artist who has already done so. Setting up a studio is a very broad and technical subject, and there are numerous books and articles available on the topic. There are also hundreds of courses available for anyone who is interested; see Q for Qualifications for details of how to find them. See over for a few self-help options to get you started.

FAST TRACK TIP FOR HOME RECORDING

'Home recording has never been so easy,' says Kian Egan of Westlife. 'Mark Feehily is brilliant at making full production backing tracks on his computer – an Apple Mac. He brings in strings, brass, piano – whatever he wants – and he does it all on a keyboard. He makes a really great-sounding demo. After seeing what he can do, I've started playing around on the computer too. I find a software program called GarageBand really great. It's only for use on a Mac computer, but if I can use it, it's very easy to use!'

FAST TRACK TO MUSIC RECORDING SKILLS

There are many courses and qualifications in music recording for those who want to gain experience or even find employment in the field. Check out the Music Education Directory, which lists recognized music courses in the UK and Ireland. Log on to www.bpi-med.co.uk, select your region and then select 'All', because for some reason the search doesn't bring up all possible options when you try to narrow it down.

Other useful sites include www.futureproducers.com and Electronic Musician at www.emusician.com. You can also check out the site of the music recording magazine Sound on Sound at www.soundonsound.com, although it's a bit overwhelming for beginners.

FAST TRACK BUDGET TIP

Reduce the cost of setting up your own recording studio by finding second-hand equipment. Check out the small ads in music magazines or publications like Loot – www.loot.com – in the UK, or Buy and Sell – www.buyandsell.ie – in Ireland. Much of it will be genuinely good-value recording equipment from people who are upgrading to more expensive wares. Do beware, as it may also be worn or broken: arrange to spend some time trying it out before handing over your hard-earned cash.

HOW DO I RECORD COVER VERSIONS OF SONGS?

If you plan to record other people's songs and sell these records, you have to pay an upfront fee to the MCPS (see C for Collection Societies). Songwriters own mechanical copyright, and every time a song is pressed and sold on CD, they receive royalties (see C for Copyright). You notify the MCPS of your intention to manufacture a record by filling out an AP2 form. They identify the correct copyright owners (the publisher and composer), and you must list them beside the song title on the sleeve of the record. The same applies if you sample part of a song written by someone else.

HOW MUCH DO I PAY THE MCPS?

If you are selling a CD of cover versions directly to fans on your website or at a live venue, you must pay the MCPS an upfront fee of 4.92 per cent of the retail price. The MCPS calculates the sum you owe them by multiplying the retail price by the number of records you are manufacturing. If you plan a print run of 1,000 CDs of ten cover songs and plan to sell them for £10, then the sum of £492 has to be paid to the MCPS before any manufacturing licence is granted. But, if only one of the ten songs is a cover version, you divide that sum by ten and pay £49.20 upfront. Paying cash upfront can be a problem for any artist or small label. However, the MCPS does make an allowance for demos or promotional copies of the CD marked with a notice saying 'Promotional Copy – Not for Sale'. See D for Demos. Incidentally, record companies pay the MCPS 8.5 per cent of the PPD (published price to dealer), which is the wholesale price. Contact the MCPS in the UK on (020) 7580 5544 or **www.mcps-prs-alliance.co.uk**; or in Ireland on (01) 676 6940 or **www.mcps.ie**.

WHAT IF I'M RELEASING MY OWN MUSIC?

If you're recording and releasing original songs, you will receive an exemption from the MCPS. You still have to fill out an AP2 form every time you release a record, but you won't be expected to pay. You will need to join the MCPS, however, in case anyone else records your music and you want to receive mechanical royalties. (See C for Collection Societies.)

HOW MUCH DOES IT COST TO PRESS A CD?

So, you've recorded an album in your bedroom. What next? You can make the tracks available as a download from your website, but you may also want to make hard copies available for review, to send to record companies, and to sell at your gigs or on your website. There are hundreds of companies who press and duplicate CDs, and the more you buy, the less it will cost per unit, so shop around. Media Shack in the UK provides a package of 1,000 CDs for £599, including VAT, at **www.mediashack.co.uk**. In Ireland, 1,000 CDs will cost €805 from **www.cd.duplication.ie**. You'll find listings of pressers and duplicators in the directories in D for Directories and on **www.yell.com** in the UK and **www.goldenpages.ie** in Ireland.

FAST TRACK TO GETTING YOUR DIY CD OUT THERE

Check out CDBaby.com – the largest online record store selling CDs direct from independent musicians. It warehouses CDs, sells them and pays artists directly. In a regular record or distribution deal, musicians can end up with just £1 per CD months, or even years, later. When selling through CD Baby, they can make £3 – 6 per CD, and get paid weekly.

There are currently 184,888 artists at CD Baby. The charge is $35 (£17.50) to have your CD selling worldwide on cdbaby.com, Apple iTunes, Yahoo Music, Best Buy, Rhapsody, MSN Music and to over 2,400 traditional retail CD stores in the US. They will keep a 9% cut of your income from digital download sales, paying the remaining 91% directly to the artist. For physical CDs, they keep $4 (£2) per CD sold.

LESS IS MORE

> *People said we were wasting our time. They said, go get real jobs. My parents threw me out. We said, hey, look, we did this album.*
>
> Geezer Butler of Black Sabbath

SINGER-SONGWRITER DAVID GRAY hit the jackpot with his demo. He managed to get a copy into the hands of Polydor's A&R man, Rob Holden. Holden was so impressed that he promptly resigned from Polydor to become Gray's manager. Now that's what I call making an impression!

I receive an average of one hundred demos a week, more than 5,000 a year. Do I listen to them? Yes, some of them. If the demo comes with a good photo and is presented professionally, my interest is usually piqued enough to listen to it. However, unless I hear something I like immediately, I'll be on to the next within seconds.

FAST TRACK TIP

The word 'demo' is short for a 'demonstration' of your music talent. You usually have a maximum of twenty seconds to make an impression, so make sure you demonstrate your talent quickly by putting the best bit of your best track right at the start of your CD.

DEMOS FOR SOLO SINGERS

Solo singers will need a demo that displays their extraordinary vocals. Select two songs that you love, that you're comfortable with and that show off your voice. Steer clear of songs from the great divas and soul legends, and choose songs that are a bit unusual, or take a classic track and put your individual stamp on it.

NO BAND, NO WORRIES

If you don't have a band to record with, you don't need to go to the expense of hiring musicians and a recording studio; simply record your demo using backing tracks. See B for Backing Tracks.

Actually '78 was a really exciting time for U2. We had just discovered F sharp minor. So we had the fourth chord and we'd only had three up to then.

Bono

DO I NEED PERMISSION TO RECORD A DEMO OF COVER SONGS?

You will need a licence from the MCPS. The society makes an allowance for demos, and charges just £20 in the UK or €30 in Ireland to record up to ten cover songs and press 500 units.

Remember: these demos can only be given away. You can't sell these recordings at your gigs or on your website. See D for DIY for more details on how to get permission to sell CDs of cover versions. See C for Collection Societies for more details about the MCPS.

DEMOS FOR SINGER-SONGWRITERS

If you're selling your songwriting ability, a simple acoustic recording with accompaniment by piano or guitar will be sufficient if the songs are strong enough. Smaller studios with one or two resident musicians can help a singer-songwriter put together the music they need for a demo at a reasonable cost. If you need to hire additional musicians and session singers, the cost will quickly escalate.

If you are looking for pop production values, you may need to bring in other professionals. Alternatively, your average computer whiz may be able to do the job for you in their home studio. See D for DIY.

CAN I RECORD A DEMO AT HOME?

If you have a studio set up at home and you know what you're doing, of course you can record at home. Many songwriters and bands record their own music and produce excellent quality recordings. However, if you're a singer and want to showcase your voice, you may be better off going to a recording studio where an engineer can make your vocals really stand out.

HOW MUCH WILL A STUDIO COST?

There are huge differences in recording studio costs. Local studios in the UK charge around £200 per day, and some offer complete demo packages for around £350. Prices in Ireland vary considerably, but, as a guide, Asylum Studios on Dublin's Abbey Street charges €350 per day. Allow at least two days to record and mix your average demo.

FAST TRACK TO FINDING A STUDIO

Ask other artists to recommend studios, and talk to people in local music shops or record stores. You'll find listings of recording studios on the business directory site www.yell. com in the UK, or www.goldenpages.ie in Ireland. Or see D for Directories.

FAST TRACK TO A SUCCESSFUL DEMO

★ Don't even think about recording a demo until you're already a polished act and have some cracking good songs.

★ Pick just two of your best songs for the demo. Less is more.

★ Put your best song first, with the catchy hook, stunning vocals or soaring chorus out in front. Shorten or omit the intro so you get to the best bit within seconds.

★ A great demo is key, but you still need the right packaging to entice people to play it. See P for Press Pack.

★ The blunderbuss approach to sending out demos is useless. See chapters on A&R, Agents, Producers, Promoters, Publishers and Record Companies for details on how to get your demo to the people who matter.

ARTIST'S LITTLE HELPERS

> *Skill is fine and genius is splendid, but the right contacts are more valuable than either.*
>
> Arthur Conan Doyle

THE INTERNET IS cluttered with music websites providing free listings of record companies, publishers and venues; I have included details of many of them throughout this book. If you want a list of contacts for the entire music industry in one place, you need to get your hands on one of several directories that are published in the UK and Ireland. The downside is that these directories are expensive, but if the cost is too much, drop in to your local library, which may provide free access to one or more of these one-stop-shop reference books.

▶ Let your fingers do the walking to find fame like Madonna's.

MUSIC WEEK DIRECTORY

This Who's Who of UK music contains more than 10,000 entries detailing record companies, music publishers, managers, recording studios and venues. It is a sister publication of the weekly magazine *Music Week*, which has been around for the last forty years. You can access much of the directory free on the magazine's website, although registration is necessary.

The directory costs £65 or is included in the cost of an annual subscription to *Music Week*, which costs £199. Go to **www.musicweek.com**; phone **(01858) 438816**.

MIM (*MUSIC INDUSTRY MANUAL*)

This 735-page directory is aimed at the UK dance music industry and focuses on dance producers and DJs. It includes the usual UK and international listings: nightclub venues, equipment, labels, shops, distributors and promoters. It also features articles on how to press up a record and how to build a club. It costs €49.95 from **www.mim.dj**.

THE UNSIGNED GUIDE

This book has 872 pages filled with 11,500 music contacts across the UK. It's aimed at unsigned bands and musicians.

The guide is available on a free seven-day trial, with a purchase price of £36.25. Order at **www.theunsignedguide.com**; phone **(0161) 907 0029**.

INTERNATIONAL SHOWCASE MUSIC BOOK

The International Showcase guide aims to be 'the bible' for professionals within the music industry. It lists studios, producers, equipment suppliers, record companies, publishers, management, promoters, venues, tour support services, and more. It also contains an artists' index of 7,000 performers.

It's available for £70, with a £20 discount for students. Go to **www.showcase-music. com**; phone **(020) 8973 3400**.

THE WHITE BOOK

This is not so much a music directory as an annual event and entertainment listings guide. It contains details of thousands of entertainment agencies, agents, performers, promoters, event organizers, lighting companies – everything you need to organize any event yourself or to target those putting on events. If you are an artist who is performing live, you can get listed in it for free.

The White Book costs £90 and is available at **www.whitebook.co.uk**; phone **(024) 7657 1176**.

CONTACTS

This handbook is published by The Spotlight and is aimed at people working in or looking to get started in the UK entertainment industry. The 2007 edition contains revised listings for over 5,000 companies, services and individuals across all branches of television, stage, film and radio. It features advice for artists starting out, including insights from leading industry professionals. It can help if you're looking for an agent or casting director, a theatre or rehearsal room, a photographer or voice coach, wigs or props.

It costs £11.50, with postage and packing costing £3.50 in the UK. Order online at **www.spotlightcd.com**; phone **(020) 7440 5032**.

THE *HOT PRESS YEARBOOK*

This reasonably priced guide to the Irish music industry contains listings of everything from PR companies and promoters to pluggers and record companies. The content is also available on the website if you subscribe.

The *Hot Press Yearbook* costs €19.95, or €16.95 if you order online at **www.hotpress.com**.

Earnings

EARNINGS
SHOW ME THE MONEY!

> There are two sorts of artists left: those who endorse Pepsi and those who simply won't.
>
> Annie Lennox

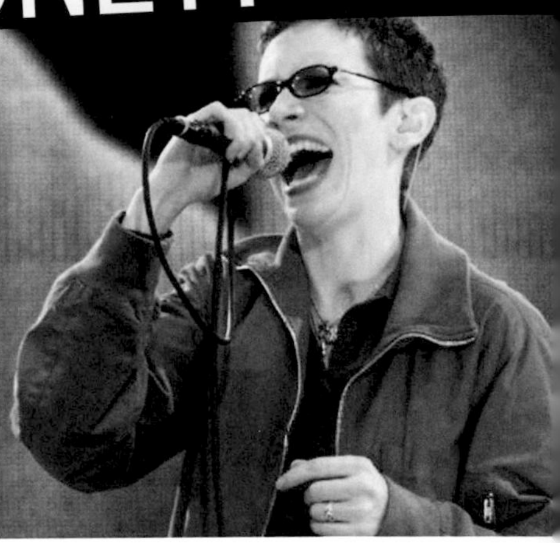

LET'S IMAGINE FOR an instant that your pop dream has come true. You've been signed by a top record company for £250,000, your début album is about to be released and your first ever single has soared to Number 1. Roll out the red carpet, crack open the bubbly and call the car dealer to order that Ferrari – you've hit the jackpot, right?

Wrong.

In fact, you've never been in so much debt in your life. At this stage in your career, you probably owe your record company somewhere in the region of £1 million.

Of course, success stories such as Robbie Williams, Christina Aguilera, U2 and Westlife make the world of pop and rock seem like a pretty appealing place for many young people. In the past few years, hundreds of thousands have flocked to auditions for shows such as *X Factor*, *Fame Academy*, *Pop Idol* and *Popstars* in the hope of being the next chart topper. And why not?

Sure, the rewards of fame and chart success can be rich. Limousines, private planes, designer clothes and five-star hotels appear to be the everyday trappings of a successful pop star's lifestyle. However, only one in many thousands of artists will reach the heady heights of superstardom. And even fewer will make the fabled amounts of money associated with legendary artists such as U2, the Rolling Stones and Paul McCartney. Even for those few who do enjoy the heady heights of success, the music business can be a precarious one.

There are artists who have sold millions of records in the United States and who have still been forced to declare bankruptcy. Hit American band TLC and US singer Toni Braxton both went broke. Another salutary tale is that of Florence Ballard from sixties legends The Supremes. She enjoyed ten Number 1 hits in the United States, but was on welfare support when she died in 1976, aged just thirty-two.

So how do pop stars make their money, and what are the pitfalls that cause them to lose it?

THE ADVANCE

Let's return to your pop dream, when you signed with the record company for £250,000.

The sum of £250,000 is a very respectable advance for a new artist today; many artists receive a significantly smaller advance. However, the sky's the limit if you're a successful superstar renegotiating a record contract: **Robbie Williams reputedly signed his last contract for a massive £80 million.**

Westlife received a pretty hefty advance of £250,000 back in 1998, although it helped that their manager had a track record that included steering Boyzone to pop fame and fortune.

Anyway, if you're lucky enough to get signed and receive an advance, don't book that Caribbean cruise just yet. This is not your personal pocket money. Consider it no more than an overdraft facility from your record company. Let's look at how quickly this advance disappears.

ROYALTIES

There's wealth and then there's superstar wealth among chart-topping music artists. Even really successful pop acts like Westlife, Kylie Minogue and Britney Spears can never hope to make the tens of millions earned by music legends such as U2 and the Rolling Stones.

Why? Because they're not songwriters.

Put simply, British singer-songwriter James Blunt will make many times more money than Australian songbird Kylie, even if they sell the same number of albums, because he will make far more in royalties.

Once upon a time, legendary singers like Frank Sinatra, Barbra Streisand and Diana Ross didn't trouble themselves with songwriting. They left that up to people called songwriters. Of course, today's artists are aware that fat royalty cheques are to be earned from having a songwriting credit on a hit track. Now even bubblegum pop acts like Britney Spears, Justin Timberlake and Jessica Simpson are suddenly displaying hitherto undiscovered songwriting skills. Their names are popping up in the credits alongside well-known lyricists, and as a result they can expect to boost their earning power considerably.

The whole issue of music royalties is a confusing one, and it's easy to get bogged down in the details. Music lawyers and accountants spend years becoming experts in this complicated arena, so here is the briefest crash course on income from royalties.

Let's pretend all music and performance royalties are one big pie. This pie is always divided into four slices. Two of the slices are filled with royalties from sales of recorded music sales – mostly CDs. The other two slices are filled with royalties earned every time this music is performed in public.

Artists who don't write their own material will get two slices of this pie. The songwriters receive the other two slices. However, the singer-songwriter, such as U2 and James Blunt, get all four slices of the royalties pie!

See also R for Royalties.

Kylie enjoys the scent of merchandising success as she launches her own perfume called Darling.

TOURING, MERCHANDISING AND ENDORSEMENTS

Artists are making more money than ever before – they're just not making as much of it from record sales.

But while record sales may be falling, ticket sales for live acts are up 25 per cent in recent years. Certainly pop acts like Kylie and Shayne Ward – who are not songwriters – make the bulk of their money from touring, merchandising and endorsements. Britney Spears and Madonna are estimated to earn 75 per cent of their money from these too.

Successful touring acts, such as Westlife and former pop stars Steps, often perform fifty dates in venues with a capacity of 10,000 fans or more. At the end of eight weeks' touring they will have earned significant amounts from ticket sales alone. These sums are not as significant as some people think as touring is expensive. However, a well-managed tour can be very lucrative. See C for Concerts to see how much money is made and how it starts to dwindle when tour expenses are subtracted.

Successful pop acts can also expect to make lucrative earnings from official merchandise, such as posters, hats and T-shirts. This can be touring merchandise or merchandise sold in high street shops or through fan clubs. Merchandising royalties are not as complicated as music royalties as they're usually based on gross sales. See M for Merchandise.

Endorsements are another lucrative source of income for successful artists. There are countless companies out there who will pay thousands – sometimes even millions – of pounds to endorse anything from Japanese beer to face creams. And there are thousands of artists who are glad to accept this source of lucre. **Elvis Presley did it back in the fifties when he advertised Southern Maid Doughnuts.** And in more recent years we've seen Britney Spears strut her stuff for Pepsi-Cola and Destiny's Child strike a pose for Wal-Mart.

If touring, merchandising and endorsements are managed properly, they're the major sources of income for many artists.

GOING, GOING, GONE: SHOW ME WHAT MONEY?

Remember the £250,000 advance from the record company? That was the good news. Now it's time for the bad news – this money is not a free gift because the label loves you; it is recoupable by the record company. However, it's not refundable. This means that it must be repaid out of future record royalties. If you are a massive pop flop and fail to make any money, it's written off along with your career.

So, an advance is like a bank overdraft facility from your record company, but the difference is the record company will write off the debt if your pop career doesn't take off. They are essentially investing in you in the hope that you will turn into a cash cow for the company.

Great, you say, if everything goes wrong. At the very least I make £250,000 in earnings. No you don't. This advance is not for a champagne and jacuzzi lifestyle. First of all, there's me to consider.

Your manager is entitled to his 20 per cent, which is £50,000. And after negotiating your record contract you will have solicitors' and accountants' fees of maybe £25,000. Need I also remind you that if you are in a band, this advance is divided between all the members of the band? If there are five of you, as there were in Westlife at the beginning, that's £35,000 apiece. And remember that you may have to live off the remainder of this money for maybe two years or more.

If you make any money from royalties and touring, it will only start to trickle down to the artist after two years. So that's an average of £17,500 per year.

Actually, I lie. The tax man will be waiting for his share of the advance, too.

This is definitely not the stuff of pink-Cadillac dreams. Although you might be able to afford a toy one, if that's any consolation.

OTHER REPAYMENTS TO THE RECORD COMPANY

Let's take it that your advance is already spent. However, you have just had a Number 1 single and you sold 500,000 copies of your début album. And let's say the terms of your contract ensure you earn £1 per album in record royalties. So – kerrching! – now you have £500,000 in the bank!

Well, not exactly. Remember that advance? That money will be recouped by the record company before they fork out a penny in record sales royalties to you. Remember, too, that the record company have spent a fortune on recording your album. All those days in the studio with the producers have racked up another £150,000 in debts.

You are also expected to pay 50 per cent of the cost of making a video to promote your single, which can average £30,000 to £50,000 for an emerging artist, to £100,000 for a bigger name. However, if you fancy a Duran Duran-style video on a yacht in the Caribbean, the sky is the limit.

After all the effort and outlay, the record company expect to lose money on the single because it's really only a promotional tool for the album. But in reality it's not the record company losing money on that single, it's you.

At the end of it all, the artist can probably only hope to get back about 4 per cent of the retail price after production costs, which can amount to just 20p per single. So if you sold 30,000 singles and reached Number 1, you would have made £6,000. Actually, you would have made only £4,800 after you have paid your manager their 20 per cent cut.

Remember the girl group B*Witched? They went straight to Number 1 with their first four singles. Their friends must have thought they had struck gold. Unfortunately, singles sales didn't translate into album sales. They worked very hard, did remarkably well for a while – even charting in America – but at the end of their few years in the business, they would have made very little money.

And we're still not at the end of your expenses. As an artist with a new album, you will also be expected to go on tour to promote this record. The record company will advance you money as tour support. However, a new act is unlikely to break even on the road. Even if you work really hard and perform in clubs, pubs and venues around the country, you may end up seriously out of pocket. You can lose £20,000 to £50,000 on a promotional tour like this.

DODGY DEALINGS

There are plenty of pitfalls for those who make it to the top of the pop world.

In the past, unscrupulous managers and promoters often creamed off more than they should, and many artists found themselves in the high court trying to claw back missing millions. These days, most budding stars will have their own personal army of accountants, music lawyers and other professionals to ensure this doesn't happen.

However, it still takes a really good accountant and music lawyer to ensure you're getting a fair deal from your record company. These professionals cost a lot of money, but when they do their jobs properly, they are worth their weight in gold.

THE ROCK 'N' ROLL LIFESTYLE

Money has a habit of disappearing when pop stars make no allowance for the fact that their career span may be a limited one. They surround themselves with excessive security and freeloading hangers-on, and spend outrageously to maintain the superstar 'image'.

The first time Boyzone appeared on *Top of the Pops*, they saw all the other artists with big, burly bouncers standing guard outside their dressing room doors. As a result they felt a little unloved because the record company hadn't provided them with beefy minders. They asked me why they were the only group at the BBC studios who didn't have their own security. I told the guys that I'd call the record company and get them as many bouncers as they wanted. I also added that they should be aware they would be paying the bouncers' salaries out of their own pockets. That was the end of the 'security' demands for a year or two, until they could afford it and actually needed it.

The following year Boyzone were back at *Top of the Pops*, and the artists with the walking barriers had disappeared off the pop scene. The bouncers made a good living, but the artists left the business with nothing.

Then there are stars like Eminem, J Lo and Mariah Carey, who are famous for their huge entourages. They like to surround themselves with heavies, make-up artists, hairstylists, family members and other hangers-on; in fact some record companies actively encourage such lavish lifestyles. What the artists don't seem to appreciate is that, ultimately, this is all coming out of their own pockets. With this rate of extravagance, even the most successful artist in the world will end up broke. Look at Michael Jackson.

 Mariah Carey with her minders.

F

Fans

FANS

CHERISH THE LOVE

The life of a rock and roll band will last as long as you can look down into the audience and see yourself.

Bruce Springsteen

WESTLIFE COULD HAVE had a real tragedy on their hands in Scotland several years ago. A teenage fan called Lynne Bowden ended up with a shocking head injury that needed seventy-six stitches. She might have died that day if our security team – which included Fran Cosgrave of *Love Island* and *I'm a Celebrity…* fame – hadn't reacted so fast.

Lynne was among hundreds of fans waiting for Westlife at a Glasgow hotel. When the tour bus arrived she was knocked over in the hysteria and cracked open her head on the kerb. Luckily, Westlife security personnel saw the incident from the bus and realized how serious it was. They bandaged her head immediately, but they estimated that she had already lost two pints of blood before the paramedics took over minutes later.

'I'll never forget that day – it was horrific,' recalls Paul Higgins, who is now Shayne Ward's tour manager. 'There was blood everywhere, we were trying to stick her forehead back and all she was concerned about was that she was getting blood on her Westlife T-shirt!'

Lynne still goes to many of the Westlife concerts today, and bears a massive scar across her forehead.

'She's quite proud of her scar,' says Higgins. 'It's like a badge of honour among Westlife fans!'

Boyzone's Keith Duffy remembers another incident in Amsterdam: 'We were rushed out of a gig and into the back of a big American van, which was like something the A-Team travelled in. I think it was a Chevrolet. It probably would have been easier if we had just signed a few autographs for the fans, but we were bundled into this van and drove off at speed. Usually the screams fade into the distance but suddenly as we were speeding down the road we realized the screaming hadn't stopped. Eventually, we copped that there must be a few fans hanging on to the big wheel that was on the back of the van. The driver didn't speak any English so he didn't know what we were trying to say to him. Then, all of a sudden, he went around a corner at speed and there were all these horrible shrieks, and then the screams faded into the distance. The driver didn't hear anything so we never did find out what happened to the screamers.'

DON'T BITE THE HAND …

We've always employed professional minders who know how to look after both the band and their fans. I can't stand the 'man mountains' employed by many of the big American acts, who routinely shove old ladies and children out of the way of 'The talent', as they refer to their artists.

Some of this behaviour can be put down to fear. After all, John Lennon, Gianni Versace and actress Rebecca Schaeffer were murdered by 'fans', but more of it is down to ego and over-zealous managers and handlers who regard fans as riff-raff. These artists seem to forget that without the fans, they have no career.

I think it's vital to treat fans with respect and appreciation.

A big factor in the success of Westlife and Shayne Ward is the amount of time they devote to meeting and greeting their fans. It's very important to be accessible and to have continual contact with fans, even when you're an established artist, and it's absolutely vital when you're starting out.

In the early days of Boyzone, music industry personnel were bewildered by how the fans always knew the exact movements of the band. Many in the music business treat occasions such as going to recording studios or appearing on TV shows as secret missions. I look on them as an opportunity to hype up the band, get people talking, and ensure that the band members meet their fans and build up die-hard devotees.

So if any of the UK or Irish fans called me – which they did all the time – I'd always give them Boyzone's schedule and tell them to pass it around. Unfortunately, fans don't follow the journalistic code of never revealing your sources. Paul Keogh, who signed Boyzone to Polygram Records in Ireland, approached a crowd of fans outside a studio one day and asked how they knew the band would be there. They all chorused: 'Louis told us!' I don't make any apologies for it, and I did the same with Westlife. It's all part of the fun of helping to break a band.

FAST TRACK FAN TIP

Signing autographs is part of being famous. If you don't want to be bothered by fans, don't become famous. Be nice to your fans, be appreciative, be gracious, sign that autograph and pose for that picture. Believe me, you'll miss them when they're gone.

EVASION TACTICS

Caution does have to be employed when checking into hotels, however, because some fans will go to any lengths to get in to their idol's room. Artists and their entourage often check in under pseudonyms to avoid getting phone calls throughout the night.

Shayne Ward's tour manager, Paul Higgins, has gone under the names Jack Hammer and Wayne Kerr. Westlife's Shane Filan has used the name Mr Woods, after his hero Tiger Woods. And Nicky Byrne must have been doing some wishful thinking when he checked in as Mr Pitt. Mark Feehily has favoured Dr Bestrong, while Kian is Mr Van Damme. 'I don't know where that name came from – I think I was put on the spot once and that's the first thing that came out,' he says.

Former Westlife heavy, Fran Cosgrave, liked to check in under the pseudonym Buzz Lightyear. On one occasion, Fran arrived in Sweden to catch up with a Westlife tour, and for some reason he had no cash, no credit card and his mobile phone was down. He had to persuade a taxi driver to take him to a hotel in Stockholm where his colleagues on the tour would be able to pay him. At the hotel he tried to check in as Buzz Lightyear. The receptionist raised an eyebrow but checked the bookings and replied that they had no reservation for a Buzz Lightyear. The manager was called and explained very slowly to 'Mr Lightyear' that he should leave now. Eventually, Fran discovered that he had gone to the wrong hotel.

FANATICAL FANS

Paul Higgins braces himself for the worst every time his acts go on tour in Asia.

'The people are truly lovely in all the countries we've visited there, but I really fear for the fans' lives sometimes,' he said. 'There seems to be little value on life and there's overcrowding in some venues and they climb up anything for a better vantage point. Public safety seems to be totally ignored. The big problem is that everyone's a fan – even the police. So instead of looking after the fans or the band, they're in the thick of it looking for autographs and photographs too! There were times when we've had to stop a performance and flee because the show was getting completely out of hand and the police were doing nothing!'

He added: 'You just don't see the same fanaticism anywhere else. I've seen kids climb fifty storeys up a fire exit to get to the band. It's crazy. I'm always afraid of serious trouble.'

Westlife's Nicky Byrne liked to check into a hotel as Mr Pitt.

G

Girls

GIRLS

THE TROUBLE WITH GIRLS

I'VE REALLY BAD news for the girls: first of all, you have a smaller chance of being signed by a record company. Then, even if you are successful, you'll probably earn far less money than the boys.

Girls are their own worst enemies in the music business. They're the ones who buy most records, go to most concerts and shell out money for T-shirts, posters and other merchandise. And girls have no problem doing that for male performers such as Take That and Justin Timberlake. However, they're much more reluctant to part with money for female acts such as Girls Aloud and the Sugababes. It's a fact – record companies know it; managers know it; agents know it.

LOWER RECORD SALES

Lower record sales are one reason why record companies are cautious about signing a female act. The Spice Girls were the only ones who managed to break the mould; they were the only girl group to inspire the same sort of hysteria and devotion that surrounds groups such as the Backstreet Boys, Westlife, Boyzone and McFly.

Girls Aloud are one of the most successful female acts out there right now. They've had fourteen consecutive Top 10 hits, which is a feat unsurpassed by any other girl group – including the Spice Girls, Diana Ross and the Supremes, Bananarama and the Sugababes. Yet Girls Aloud can never hope to match Westlife in terms of earnings and success. They can't tour like a boyband simply because they can't sell the same number of tickets. Nor can they ever hope to sell the same amount of albums or merchandise.

Compare Take That's big comeback with that of All Saints. Take That's album and tour were major success stories. All Saints, on the other hand, never, ever felt so low as when their album *Studio One* only managed to reach number 40 and they were dropped by their record company in March 2007.

HIGHER COSTS

There's another problem with female artists. Record companies are more reluctant to sign them because they cost more – much, much more.

Girls are high-maintenance pop stars.

Peelin' 'em [clothes] off is the easy cheesy way for women, but it helps if you're crap.

Dolores O'Riordan, formerly of The Cranberries

Girls Aloud are a high-maintenance group.

Maintaining a glossy, superstar image is as much an essential part of being in a girl group as the ability to dance and sing at the same time. It's all about selling the dream of ordinary girls finding fame, wealth, glamour and beauty.

Michael Jackson's hair and make-up bill while making the video *Scream* was reportedly $3,000 per day. And we all know that Michael is fond of his slap. Yet his sister Janet's hair and make-up in the same video was said to cost a whopping $8,000 a day.

And when the Backstreet Boys recorded the video *Girlfriend/Boyfriend* with Janet Jackson in 1999, their wardrobe bill amounted to $25,000 for the five of them; newspapers reported that Janet's alone cost $10,000.

Record companies know they are not going to make the same margins on a female act because they have to shell out so much money on styling, grooming and wardrobe. In fact it's make-up artists, hairdressers, stylists and fashion designers who make the big money from the girls.

CATFIGHTING

There's a common perception that behind the scenes of a girl band it's all catfights and screaming rows . . . and it's not wrong. When you spend time together in a band you become like family and, like all families, you become dysfunctional. Let's just say that girl bands are more dysfunctional than any others.

'Why is she singing lead in that song? Why is she in the middle of that photo? Why can't I wear that dress?' These are the kind of disputes every manager and record company hears from girl bands. The Sugababes have already seen two changes in their line-up, and there's only three of them. And the Spice Girls, All Saints and Eternal all split up because of in-fighting.

I'm not saying that the guys don't squabble, because they do. But there's usually some kind of power struggle going on in girl bands that makes them more fraught.

Yes, I'm afraid the girls have a bit of a bad reputation in the music business. It's up to you to change that.

The Pussycat Dolls may have huge success but will find it hard to make as much money as the big boybands.

THE GOOD NEWS
The big advantage of girls is that they're much easier to promote than the guys.

Well, they're easy to promote if they look anything like Girls Aloud, Sugababes, Pussycat Dolls, Beyoncé, Britney or Christina. Yes, the media appears to be run by dirty old men who can't get enough of pop stars with cleavage, long legs and airbrushed pouts. However, not all female artists are equal. Let's just say that the likes of Sinéad O'Connor, KD Lang and The Pointer Sisters are not likely to receive the same kind of coverage as the glossy girl acts.

Dolores O'Riordan says it's 'easy cheesy' to use your sexuality as a tool in the music business. But the 'easy cheesy' way has been successful for many women in the past. I doubt Kylie would be as big a star today if it wasn't for the storm created by those gold hot pants a few years ago. All the really successful female artists, from Beyoncé to Madonna, have never been shy about strutting their stuff.

If you've got what it takes, then use it. There's no point buttoning up, being precious and focusing on making your career last. Chances are if you don't get noticed in the first place, you won't have a career.

I put together a girl band called Bellefire a few years back. They were beautiful girls with great voices and they got not one, but two record deals. But we made the mistake of letting the second record company, Warner Music Group, persuade us to style them for 'longevity'. The record sleeve featured the girls looking like some badly dressed gypsies around a campfire. Their first single did quite well and then Warner Records selected and released the group's second single, Spin the Wheel. The whole promotion of it was a disaster. They simply shrugged and told us they couldn't get any radio stations to play the single that they had selected and released. I've never heard anything so ridiculous from a major record company. Warner Records UK is my least favourite record company. That was the end of Bellefire.

Of course, daring to bare is not the only form of exhibitionism. Another tried and tested route is to do what Lily Allen and Amy Winehouse do. It's also what Sinéad O'Connor was doing years before them: stirring up controversy. Lily is famous for expressing forthright and usually critical opinions about other musicians, but as a result she makes headlines. That doesn't guarantee record sales, but if people know you exist, your music stands a chance of being added to their record collection. Be warned that it can backfire. The first amendment and freedom of speech doesn't seem to apply to female artists. Sinéad O'Connor's career was badly damaged when she ripped up a photo of the Pope on TV, while The Dixie Chicks were pulled off radio stations in the US for bashing Bush and saying they were 'ashamed the President of the United States is from Texas'.

Yet this is not a business in which girls can be shy and retiring. The truth is, that as a female in the business, you have to use everything you've got and more to get ahead.

Amy Winehouse has successfully courted controversy for fame.

The HoaX Factor

THE HOAX FACTOR
REMEMBER: NO WORK, NO FEE!

> *A word to the wise ain't necessary; it's the stupid ones who need all the advice.*
>
> Bill Cosby

THE SUCCESS OF *X FACTOR* has contributed to the growth of what you might call the HoaX Factor. Dodgy showbiz 'agents' are conning star-struck hopefuls via bogus auditions at which they make promises of stardom in return for a large fee. Wannabe actors, models and singers have gone to so-called 'auditions' and handed over fees from £100 to £1,000 or more. These unscrupulous individuals claim to have TV jobs for aspiring actors, singers, dancers and extras, who pay hundreds of pounds to enrol in casting directories, but never receive any work.

The Advertising Standards Authority in Britain has upheld a string of complaints about dodgy agents, including one that had used the BBC's name and claimed they were recruiting for the popular TV series *Doctor Who*. The problem continues to grow because so many young people are desperate to find a route to stardom.

Since 2004, agencies have been unable to charge registration fees, but they can still charge to include artists in their casting directories. The government has now decided to review the laws covering agency fees, and is considering making it illegal to charge on-the-spot deposits at casting events.

FAST TRACK TO AVOIDING THE HOAX FACTOR

There is never a charge to attend a bona fide audition, and legitimate agents never charge money upfront. Reputable agents should use the slogan: 'no work, no fee'.Take care before registering online with any agency or so-called directory. Don't respond to advertisements that offer auditions at a hotel or similar venue for work as TV extras, singers or models.

LEGITIMATE AGENTS

Reputable agents will only sign you if they feel that you have the potential to earn money for them; they will then charge 10 per cent commission on your earnings.

Some agencies may suggest that you go to a professional photographer, who will provide you with 'a card' or photographs to be used to introduce you to clients. If there are significant costs, reputable agencies will cover these themselves and recoup the money from your future earnings.

Agents may also demand that you produce tapes and showreels. If these are submitted to a client and aren't returned, don't complain. These are your promotional tools and you are expected to provide them at your own cost.

Never go to a non-business address on your own for a meeting or audition. If you feel you must attend, tell someone where you are going or take a friend. Anyone who guarantees you work and stardom should be regarded suspiciously. There are no guarantees in this business. See A for Agents.

FAST TRACK TIP FOR COMPLAINTS

If you have paid to register with an agent or agency and haven't received any work, you can complain or receive further information at The Employment Agency Standards Inspectorate, 1 Victoria Street, London SW1H OET; eas@dti.gsi.gov.uk; or phone 0845 955 5105.

Image
Internet

I

I'M TOO SEXY FOR MY SHIRT

> *Imagine taking off your make-up and nobody knows who you are.*
>
> Steven Tyler of Aerosmith

▶ Steven Tyler strikes a pose.

YOU DON'T NEED the abs of Justin Timberlake or the legs of Christina Aguilera to achieve pop stardom – although it sure helps! **The song is the true key to success,** but the packaging comes a close second.

Image is not all about glamour, or Marilyn Manson would not be where he is. And if it was all about good looks, we'd never have heard of Shane MacGowan! Celine Dion was no oil painting in the beginning either, but she has pulled every trick in the book from getting her teeth done to airbrushing her publicity shots to creating an incredibly glossy image.

Image is about developing your own unique celebrity identity. It's about grabbing people's attention visually and holding it. As a result, the right stylist can be as important to your career as the correct record producer.

Elton John is another artist who might never be described as 'buff', but his zany spectacles, platform shoes and outrageous outfits certainly captured the public's imagination. David Bowie was also a genius in the image department, as was Elvis Presley for his time.

The power of packaging is vital where female pop acts are concerned. Girls in this business have to look impossibly sexy and glossy, yet those looks come at a high price and require the most advanced technology. An army of back-room specialists – fashion stylists, hairstylists, make-up artists, nutritionists, personal trainers and lighting technicians – produce platinum-blonde Christina Aguilera's jazz-vamp looks and sultry Beyoncé's sexy glamour-girl style. And if all else fails there's computerized digital enhancement, which could even make me look good!

And don't be fooled by the just-got-out-of-bed look so popular with rock and indie bands. The 'unstyled' look of Oasis, U2 and the Manic Street Preachers is almost as carefully contrived and staged by teams of stylists as the glamour look.

▶ Even *X Factor* winner, Shayne Ward, needs a little help in the make-up department sometimes.

Even Bono admitted he looked like sixties Greek singer, Nana Mouskouri, until he got a stylist in the late eighties.

The reality is that sex sells, and image is an important element in many fields, not just the music industry. It's crucial that you have the right look if you want to get noticed. However, it's not all about good looks, heaving bosoms, big pecs, bare midriffs and long legs. Even Kylie and her gold hot pants could never have landed her first Number 1 UK hit in ten years if 'Spinning Around' hadn't been a great little pop song.

WESTLIFE IMAGE PROBLEMS

Sony BMG boss Simon Cowell certainly didn't see the X factor in Westlife when they started out. Actually, his exact words were: 'You've got to be kidding me – some of them are really ugly!' Well, that's Simon. He's never heard that you only need to apply pressure to transform coal into diamonds. I was sure that with a bit of grooming, this bunch of teenage schoolboys would scrub up nicely as pop heart-throbs.

Top Dublin hairstylist Gary Kavanagh agreed with Simon Cowell though. Gary is the resident celebrity snipper with Peter Mark salons in Ireland, and has teased the tresses of stars such as La Toya Jackson, Celine Dion and Kylie Minogue.

'Mark Feehily looked like a street busker with shoulder-length hair, and Kian Egan looked like a complete muppet with long hair parted in the middle,' recalls Gary. 'I couldn't exactly imagine girls going gooey-eyed and dreamy over this lot. But when I started working on them, I could see they were great kids. A lot of young guys would be afraid of anyone going near their hair. Westlife didn't care what I did – I could have cut their heads off and they wouldn't have complained. You could see they had the right attitude from the start. They were eager to do whatever they had to do.'

BEAUTY: GENIUS NOT GENES

There are very few pop stars who get out of bed in the morning looking like they do in the magazines. Anyone can look great with the right styling, hair and make-up, and by paying attention to their shape and figure.

Every budding young star needs to have the discipline to get in shape if they want to succeed.

There are very few overweight pop stars, so, if weight is a problem, deal with it at this stage or forget about it. And yes, the stars do have professionals to transform them into Hollywood hunks and honeys, but you'll just have to be clever and improvise. Watch, learn, imitate and experiment, and see what works for you and your music.

FAST TRACK TO SUPERSTAR STYLING ON A BUDGET

Fashion

You may not be able to afford your own stylist, but that doesn't mean you can't use the services of a fashion adviser for free. Many of the major high street chain stores have their own personal shopper and stylist services. Topshop alone has a network of over forty trained advisers in the UK and Ireland. So too do stores such as House of Fraser, John Lewis and Harvey Nichols. Just make an appointment. They are nearly always free, there's no minimum purchase, and they could discover an entirely new you.

Make-up

There's free professional advice and even free makeovers available in the cosmetics department of many stores. You need an appointment with some consultants, but if you arrive early or on a weekday, you might be seen anyway. Visit different make-up consultants until you find a look that really suits you.

Hair

You don't need to shell out big money on a posh stylist for superstar looks. A simple wash and blow-dry at your local hairdresser will give you the glossy finish you need for auditions or interviews.

It may be worth splashing out on a really good stylist if you're making a major style change and want a completely new look. Also, hair salons look for guinea pigs or 'models' for their trainees. They are always supervised so there is usually no problem.

INTERNET

HOW TO BE FAMOUS VIRTUALLY!

When I took office, only high-energy physicists had ever heard of what is called the Worldwide Web. Now even my cat has its own Web page.

Bill Clinton

THERE'S CURRENTLY A lot of PR hype about web-driven music phenomena such as Sandi Thom, OK Go, Arctic Monkeys and Lily Allen.

It's true that aspiring music stars can now turn the traditional route to fame on its head, thanks to the 'viral' marketing nature of the internet. Many are learning to use it successfully as a launch pad for greater things.

▶ Alex Turner from The Arctic Monkeys, who used the internet as a launch pad for rock fame and fortune.

Essex rock band Koopa proved that a band doesn't even need to be signed to a record label to have a chart hit. Anyone who sells songs through approved download services became eligible for the charts in January 2007. Koopa made history as the first unsigned act to land a UK Top 40 single that same month.

However, don't overestimate the importance of the internet. Exploiting this outlet alone will not be enough to achieve real success. Despite all the hype, the music arena is still largely driven by the record companies and the media.

Nevertheless, the internet is undoubtedly a valuable and cost-effective tool for any emerging artist. So if you don't already know the basics of using the internet, then get up to speed quickly. It's one of the fastest and cheapest marketing tools an emerging artist can have. And let me add that I have helped make a little 'virtual' pop history myself. It was Westlife who landed the first Number 1 on the first official UK download music charts in September 2004 with a live version of 'Flying Without Wings'. Since then artists no longer need to sell a single CD to go to the top of the charts. Gnarls Barkley made history by becoming the first act to get a Number 1 hit on the sales of downloads alone in April 2006 with the song 'Crazy'.

Networking communities such as MySpace and Bebo now influence the way performers become famous. Many artists are bypassing record companies and radio DJs to distribute their own songs, promote themselves globally and win their own audience in cyberspace. It has proved an effective launch pad for artists like Arctic Monkeys and Lily Allen. Why shouldn't it be yours?

FAST TRACK TO SETTING UP YOUR WEBSITE

Do You Need Your Own Website?

Can you afford to set up your own website right now? If you already have an audience and something to sell, such as live shows, CDs or T-shirts, a website is great. If not, it doesn't make commercial sense to launch your own site. There are lots of free alternatives through which to make your presence felt on the internet (see below).

DIY or Pro?

If you decide to go ahead with a website, do you have the skills to create your own site or do you need to get a professional on board?

Domain registering sites such as **123-reg.co.uk** have web-building packages to help you create your own site, but you can pay anything from £80 to £300 for your package.

A web designer will charge between £300 and £500 for a standard website of about ten pages. If you want to include a fan forum and e-commerce, the cost may reach £1,000 or more.

Cee-Lo Green likes to gloat that his act Gnarls Barkley were the first ever to go to Number 1 on sales of downloads alone.

Get Your Domain Name

If you go the DIY route you will need your own domain name; most web designers will include this as part of their package. See N for Naming Your Act. Remember that there are big price differences between domain registrars. With **123-reg.co.uk**, the domain name **louiswalsh.com** is priced at £8.99 a year, **louiswalsh.co.uk** is priced at £2.59 and **louiswalsh.eu** is £14.95. At **register.ie** in Ireland, **louiswalsh.com** costs €14.99 per year, **louiswalsh.ie** costs a whopping €96.79 and **louiswalsh.eu** costs €24.99.

Hosting

Hosting companies provide the storage space and services you need to run your website. Most domain registering services also offer hosting, so it may be easier to get both together. Talk to people who have websites and see if they are happy with their hosting service and the level of customer support. Hosting services cost anything from £30 to £150 or more per year.

Maintenance

There's no point going to the expense of setting up a website unless you are going to maintain and update it regularly. There's nothing more frustrating for fans than an out-of-date website. Make sure your email address is included or that you feature a fans' forum on the site. Feedback is a very important and valuable part of having a website.

FAST TRACK TO GAINING VIRTUAL 'FRIENDS'

Keep your website or MySpace site up to date with a daily blog. Boldface or highlight the names of fans, or anyone in the music business, that you encounter; people will then keep checking the site to see if they are mentioned. When their names appear, they will invariably pass the link to everyone else they know and your traffic should grow and grow. When you can show that you have acquired a large number of 'friends', record companies will suddenly become more interested.

E TEAMS AND STREET TEAMS

eTeams are groups of fans who spread the word about a band online. They talk-up the artist or band on chat and message sites through email, etc. Street teams are groups of fans who work together to promote a band on the streets. This can be by handing out fliers, selling tickets for shows, or calling radio shows and requesting airplay for their favourite band's new single.

Having your own web presence enables you to mobilize motivated fans to promote you and your products. In return, you can reward team members with exclusive news, tickets or merchandise of the band. Ask for help and you may be surprised how many are willing to give it. For free!

FAST TRACK SITES TO VIRTUAL FAME

YouTube.com

More than 100 million videos are watched per day on the internet video site YouTube. The company's slogan is 'Broadcast Yourself', and it allows people to watch and share original videos or podcasts worldwide.

You don't need a multi-million-pound budget to make your mark on this site. See V for Video to find out how American rockers OK Go managed to make the most downloaded video in history on a $10 budget. Other video-sharing sites include **iFilm. com**, **tv.blinx.com**, **video.google.com**, **video.yahoo.com**, **flickr.com** and **revver.com**.

MySpace.com

MySpace is the biggest social networking site out there, with 95 million registered users. If it was a country, it would be the twelfth biggest in the world. It is particularly attractive for music artists because it makes it very easy for users to show, edit and share music and videos. The site is a great way for you, as an unsigned artist, to promote your music and interact with fans.

Of course, the next logical step is to start selling music, and MySpace plan to enable artists to sell downloads of their original music, turning budding artists into online music retailers.

Bebo

Bebo is a social networking site rivalling the web giant MySpace. It was listed as the second most popular site in Ireland last year. In July 2006 it responded to the popularity of MySpace in the music community by launching Bebo Bands, where bands and solo artists are able to create a homepage showcasing their music.

Other Online Sites

Xanga.com is a popular networking site for music fans and artists. **Purevolume.com** and **AbsolutePunk.net** are popular sites on which American punk and hardcore fans communicate, and struggling bands post free files for sampling. **Facebook.com** is the leading social networking site among college students in America, and more recently in the UK and Ireland. It's great for posting notices of gigs and, like **Friendster.com** and many other networks, it now facilitates music downloads with its iLike feature. Users must register using a school or business email.

VIRTUAL FAME FAST TRACKERS

My Chemical Romance

American outfit My Chemical Romance set out on the path to fame by offering free downloads at **Purevolume.com**. They also built up a cult following on MySpace, where they gathered 100,000 'friends' before coming to the attention of record companies and getting themselves signed.

The Libertines

Pete Doherty's old band, The Libertines, were among the first to harness the power of the internet to spread their music. They frequently posted on fan forums, and Doherty used his own blog to communicate with fans. They also regularly released songs free on the internet.

Arctic Monkeys

The Arctic Monkeys built up a huge fan base on the MySpace website, according to the official spin. As a result, **their first album, *Whatever People Say I Am*, released in 2005, became the fastest-selling début album in UK chart history.** A different version of the story is that they handed out fifty CDs to fans at the early shows; these fans started file sharing and that's how their music and popularity spread.

Sandi Thom

Sandi has entered the annals of internet music lore. Her début track, 'I Wish I Was A Punk Rocker', went to Number 1 after she successfully created a 'buzz' online. The story goes that she decided to broadcast her concerts via a webcam from her basement in South London, because her car kept breaking down on the way to gigs. After two weeks she had amassed an audience of 162,000 – larger than Wembley Stadium. I'm sure there's a little record label embellishment in the tale, but she still ended up signing a million-pound contract with Sony. Of course, the deal was signed live via her webcam.

Lily Allen

UK singer Lily Allen has been described as the poster girl for the MySpace generation. She placed four songs on her MySpace page, there was a flurry of file sharing and she ended up with 25,000 'friends'. The truth is that Allen was actually signed to Parlophone before she put up the site. Still, she successfully used the internet to generate lots of interest in advance of her début album, *Alright Still*.

FAST TRACK TIP TO VIRTUAL FAME: SELLABAND.COM

Want to invest in the next U2, or better still do you want to be the next U2? A Dutch-based company called Sellaband.com may just be able to help you. This site was launched in August 2006 and allows music fans or 'believers' to invest in unsigned acts.

Each 'believer' can invest increments of $10, and if you manage to find 5,000 believers and $50,000, you get access to a recording studio and professional production, songwriting and marketing expertise. Or you can find 2,500 believers who will buy two shares, or even one rich believer who will buy all 5,000 shares – you get the drift.

Basically, bands and their believers go into business together on this site. All revenue generated via advertising and CD sales is shared equally between artists, their believers and Sellaband.com. The company also makes money from the interest on funds, which are held in trust until an act manages to collect $50,000.

Sellaband.com is yet another internet route to financing your music and getting it out to people.

Jobs
Journalists
and Media

J

JOBS
GIS A JOB!

SO YOU'RE A music artist. Simply labelling yourself as such doesn't give you a licence to do nothing until the world recognizes your genius. Most budding stars have to spend a long time auditioning, rehearsing, studying, learning and working until they get their big break. Some of you will already be lucky or talented enough to earn a good living from gigging and performing. You may have an agent and a manager and be well on the way to international fame and fortune.

Others will not be so lucky.

If you're sitting around waiting to be discovered, you might just find yourself sitting around for a long, long time! The truth is, you have a greater chance of being discovered if you are out there in the workplace, meeting people. Hanging around, refusing to compromise your artistic integrity and playing the starving-artist-in-the-garret role is isolating and unhelpful. Brian McFadden was a security guard for a burger chain; Shayne Ward worked in a store in the Arndale Shopping Centre, Manchester, while also part of pop trio Destiny; and long after Boyzone was formed, Ronan Keating still worked in Korky's shoe shop in Dublin. Any job is better than no job.

WHAT SORT OF JOB?

It's a bonus if you can find employment in a field that's related to your music aspirations. Working for a record company, for example, will give you an insight into the music industry. **A job in a theatre, a live music venue or radio station will also allow you to learn as you earn,** and at the same time make valuable contacts in other entertainment and media industries.

Have an open mind about where you want to work, because no experience is ever wasted. Do whatever it takes to get your foot in the door, because once you have a job, any job, enthusiasm and a hard work ethic will get you to places you want to be. My first job was as a messenger boy for Irish show band manager, Tommy Hayden Enterprises. I learned the business from the ground up, and that's the best way to do it. Simon Cowell started out in the mail room of EMI Publishing. Everyone I know who is really successful in the music business started at the bottom and clawed their way up.

FAST TRACK TO WORK EXPERIENCE

P Diddy – known variously as Puff Daddy, Diddy and Sean John Combs – claims he was the first 'intern' in the music industry in America. He got the job he wanted by targeting Uptown Records, calling them every day, and offering to work for free. Clearly

P. Diddy started out as an intern in a record company and now owns one.

he was a quick learner, as he now runs a hip hop music empire from his own record label, Bad Boy Records.

Unfortunately, work experience involves no pay, low pay or sometimes just travel expenses. Also, these work placements in the music industry and related media are rarely advertised and hard to find.

FAST TRACK TIPS TO WORK EXPERIENCE

[1] Believe it or not, you need experience to land work experience. Read Sony BMG's tips for applying for their jobs at www.sonybmg.co.uk. Working in a record store or a respected live music venue is a great start, as is DJing on your local or student radio station. Why not write music reviews for the local freesheet or student magazine?

[2] Research the record companies or music publishing companies that look after artists you really admire and who produce music that you're really passionate about. Learn everything you can about the company; their website is usually the best place to start.

[3] The next step is to find out who to contact in that company. Call the company and find out who deals with work experience applications. Get a name, get a title, get an email address, and make sure you get the correct spelling.

[4] Send your expertly crafted CV and cover letter to this person directly. If you hear nothing back from him or her within ten days, try sending it again by post. Emails are easily deleted or forgotten about.

[5] Still nothing? Not surprising. This is where persistence is called for. Try a phone call. You'll probably end up leaving a message: tell them who you are, what you're calling about, and ask if they would consider seeing you for five minutes.

[6] Try again, but always be pleasant, courteous, and don't cross the line from being persistent to becoming a pest. Be especially nice to record company PAs (personal assistants). They hold the keys to a lot of doors.

FAST TRACK TO COVER LETTERS

The cover letter accompanies a CV. It should be brief. You probably shouldn't emphasize that your real ambition is to be a pop superstar when the only opening they have is in the mail room. But make it clear that the music business is your passion.

Opposite is an example of a cover letter, in which the applicant (me) is applying to A. N. Other in Number One Records. There is absolutely no point in sending applications to Simon Cowell, Lucian Grainge or the managing director of any big record company; it will never get beyond their assistants and will end up in the bin. Pick up the phone, find out the name of the person who deals with job applications and send it directly to them.

Louis Walsh
Wannabe
Very Eager
Dublin

A. N. Other
Number One Records
Easy Street
London

1 October 2007

Dear Mr Other,

(1. Introduce yourself and explain why you are sending this CV.)
I am 21 years old *(no sniggering)* and I am writing to you because I would really love to secure work experience with Number One Records. I'm more than happy to work in an unpaid position in exchange for learning more about this company and the music business.

(2. Outline your relevant education – state whether you are a graduate or have studied music etc., and any skills you've acquired such as DJing or reviewing bands.)
My passion is music and I've been managing my own band called Time Machine. I have also had experience working in Tommy Hayden's music management company as a messenger boy. I feel I have enough basic experience to be of help around the office, but I welcome the opportunity to learn more.

(3. Show that you have some knowledge of and genuine interest in the company you are applying to.)
I really admire your label's incredible success with Bird Brain and Bad Butterflies, and really want to learn from a company that I regard as the best in the pop business.

(4. Wrap it up.)
I have attached my CV, but if you need any further information, please feel free to contact me. I look forward to hearing from you.

Yours sincerely,
Louis Walsh

FAST TRACK TIP TO A PERFECT CV

There are many sample CVs out there, and all of them vary in style or content. For a good example of a performer's CV, go to the Skillset Careers website at www.skillset.org/careers. Do a search for 'hints and tips' – it's tricky to find otherwise – and there you'll find a great step-by-step guide to writing the perfect CV.

FAST TRACK TO A MEDIA JOB

It's not always easy to find work in the music business. However, there are many related industries, such as TV, film and radio, which will provide valuable experience and contacts for a budding music star.

Skillset Careers is a free advice and guidance service for the media industry, dealing with everyone from students and new entrants to experienced media professionals. It has dedicated media career helplines staffed by specialist advisers who will give you general advice and information about careers, education and training. They also offer one-to-one career guidance with CV and self-marketing advice.

The helpline 08080 300 900 (England, Wales and Northern Ireland) is staffed from 8 a.m. to 10 p.m., seven days a week. The helpline 0808 100 8094 (Scotland) is staffed from 8 a.m. to 8 p.m., Monday to Friday. The careers service coordinator is also available on (020) 7520 5757. Visit the Skillset Careers website at www.skillset.org/careers.

The Northern Visions Media Centre in Belfast offers training courses in video, sound recording and editing at reasonable prices. Visit them at Northern Visions Media Centre, 23 Donegal Street, Belfast BT1 2FF; www.northernvisions.org; phone (028) 9024 5495.

FAS/Screen Training Ireland offers training courses for those wishing to pursue a career in film, TV and digital media. Its website has a section on how to get started, and also offers bursaries for trainees in the industry. See www.screentrainingireland.ie; phone (01) 483 0840.

FAST TRACK TO JOB LISTINGS AND OPPORTUNITIES IN MUSIC AND MEDIA

Record Companies

See R for Record Companies for contact details for both 'major' and 'indie' labels. Check out the jobs section on Sony BMG's website at **www.sonybmg.co.uk**, which gives details of what they're looking for in applicants. However, don't just apply to the four majors. You might get more valuable experience at a smaller indie label.

Job Centre Plus

Do a search for jobs for singers, DJs, dancers or musicians on this government site and you'll be surprised at what pops up all over the UK. See **www.jobseekers.direct.gov.uk**.

Stage

The Spice Girls all answered an advert placed in *Stage* magazine. The recruitment section is the standard way to find auditions for professional singers, dancers, Caribbean cruise and red coat entertainers, and even record labels. See **www.thestage.co.uk**.

Music Magazines

Check out the jobs section in *Music Week*, which advertises vacancies for everything from record label receptionist to record company manager. You can also see the jobs online at **www.musicweek.co.uk** and **www.gigmag.co.uk**. Why not get a job at *Music Week*, or indeed any music magazine? *Hit Sheet* is a terrific UK music magazine with a CD that comes out every fortnight, previewing and promoting great music. See **www.hitsheet.co.uk**. In Ireland, try *Hot Press* at **www.hotpress.com** and *Rap Ireland* magazine at **www.rapireland.com**.

The *Guardian*

Log on to the media section of the *Guardian*'s job adverts for hundreds of vacancies in fields associated with music. Also, read the *Media Guardian* supplement, which is published with the paper every Monday. See **www.guardian.co.uk**.

Street Teams and eTeams

Many A&R people and music journalists start out as members of street teams and eTeams who promote bands by handing out fliers, talking them up on chat forums, requesting airplay on radio shows, etc. This is not a paid job, but it can give you a foot in the door. See Roadrunner Records, for example, who recruit and run their own street teams at **www.roadrunnerrecords.co.uk**.

Disney

Disney hires thousands of performers every year, and even landed the number one spot on *US Business Week*'s inaugural 'Best Place to Launch a Career'. It's difficult to get an Employment Authorization Document (EAD) to take up employment in the US, however there are visas such as the J-1 that allow students to work there during the summer. There's also Disneyland Paris for those who can speak French, or check out Disney Cruise Lines. See **www.disney.com/careers** or **www.disneylandparis-casting.com**.

Cruise Ships

Musicians, bands and singers are required by cruise lines all over the world. Some cruise companies recruit entertainers themselves – look at their websites and follow the links for career prospects with the company. The most common route is through agencies such as Sixth Star Entertainment & Marketing in Florida, which specializes in providing entertainment for many of the top cruise companies. They have an excellent website on which the details of their application process are featured. See **www.sixthstar.com**; phone **(001) 954 462 6760**.

Music Publishers' Association

Job vacancies in the industry are advertised on this site, and the Association also holds induction courses three times a year, allowing an insight into the business of music publishing. See **www.mpaonline.org.uk**.

Radio

Surround yourself in music and sound and familiarize yourself with sound studios by working in radio. You can find and browse all local, regional and national English, Scottish, Welsh and Northern Irish radio stations on **www.radio-now.co.uk**. You use their clickable maps and UK radio station directory to find the stations near to you.

A list of the 58 independent national, local and community stations in Ireland is available on the Broadcasting Commission of Ireland's site at **www.bci.ie**.

Broadcast Now

This site advertises jobs from runners in TV companies to video producers, engineers and sound supervisors. See **www.broadcastnow.co.uk**.

Mandy

This is a free recruitment site for film and TV companies. However, it does also feature adverts for everything from extras for music videos in London to male dancers in Dublin. See **www.mandy.com**.

Nemesis Casting

Former Take That manager Nigel Martin Smith runs this TV casting and model agency in Manchester. You can send a photograph and CV, along with an SAE, to **New Recruits, Nemesis Casting, Nemesis House, 1 Oxford Court, Bishopsgate, Manchester M2 3WQ**; or apply online at **www.nemesiscasting.co.uk**.

Film TV Extra

This is a free site containing details of castings for extras and adverts, as well as lists of both English and Irish agents and casting directors. See **www.filmtvextra.com**.

Subscription Sites

Star Now is a recruitment site with vacancies for singers on cruise liners, dancers in a five-star hotel in Mexico and MTV reality TV contestants. It carries listings for the UK, Ireland and America. I wouldn't normally include a site like this because it has a subscription charge, but you can still register and browse for free. However, complete access to the site costs £9.95 for a one-month subscription or £23.70 for six months. See **www.starnow.com**. Or check out The Casting Studio at **www.thecastingstudio.co.uk**, which has an annual subscription of £36.95 per year.

Reality TV in America

Spread your wings a little bit with this site, where you can find out who's hiring in America. Casting details are available for hundreds of reality TV shows, including MTV programmes, *America's Next Top Model*, *Extreme Makeover* and *Jerry Springer*. See **www.realitytvcastingcall.com**. A similar site is **www.realityshows.com**. Remember that you need the appropriate visa and EAD (Employment Authorization Document) to be able to work in the US and this can be difficult to get.

The Music Market

This is a recruitment agency for music, film and new media industries. See **www.the musicmarket.co.uk**; phone **(020) 7486 9102**.

CAT Entertainment

This is a recruitment agency for the TV, home entertainment, film and music industries. Clients include Universal Studios TV, MTV, Paramount, Nickelodeon and Fox Kids. See **www.njdgroup.co.uk**; phone **(01753) 630040**.

Rose Inc.

Another headhunting agency in the entertainment industry. Clients include Channel 4, The Ministry of Sound and MTV. See **www.rose-music.co.uk**; phone **(020) 7836 2666**.

Musicians.co.uk

Join this free database of musicians, including DJs, songwriters, producers, session musicians and so on, which is aimed at potential employers. See **www.musicians.co.uk**.

BBC

The BBC has a jobs page advertising vacancies for everything from receptionists to producers, as well as information on applying for work experience. Contact **PO Box 7000, London W1A 8GJ**; email **recruitment@bbc.co.uk**; or see **www.bbc.co.uk/jobs**.

ITV

Foot-in-the-door vacancies such as production runners are advertised, as are jobs for presenters, reporters and researchers. See **www.itvjobs.com**.

BSkyB

This website contains details of vacancies, including work experience available in Sky News and other areas of the business. Contact **Human Resources, Grant Way, Isleworth, Middlesex TW7 5QD**; email **skyjobs@bskyb.com**; see **www.sky.com/jobs**; phone **0870 240 3000**.

Channel 4

Information on vacancies and work experience is available on the website. Contact **Channel 4, 124 Horseferry Road, London SW1P 2TX**; or see **www.channel4.com/4careers**.

Discovery Channel

See **www.discoverychannel.co.uk** for information on job opportunities with one of the largest makers of factual programming in the world.

The History Channel

A limited number of job opportunities are listed on this website. Contact **The History Channel, Grant Way, Isleworth, Middlesex TW7 5QD**; see **www.thehistorychannel.co.uk**; phone **(020) 7705 3000**.

MTV

Email **internship@mtvne.com** or see **www.mtv.co.uk** for information on applying for work or work experience with MTV Europe.

RTE

Check for vacancies in the online jobs section of this national Irish radio and TV station. See **www.rte.ie/about/jobs**.

TV3

This commercial Irish station has a careers section online. See **www.tv3.ie**.

UTV

This Northern Irish TV station has a careers page online. Contact **UTV Plc, Ormeau Road, Belfast BT7 1EB**; see **www.utvinternet.ie**; phone **(028) 9026 2177**.

OTHER

See L for Live Performing for other ideas on how to get started in the business.

> *Just because it's in print doesn't mean it's the gospel. People write negative things 'cause they feel that's what sells. Good news to them, doesn't sell.*
>
> Michael Jackson

IT'S COMMON FOR celebrities to whinge about the 'intrusion' of the media. **If you don't want press attention, go and get a job in a supermarket where you're guaranteed a paparazzi-free lifestyle.** If you want to be a pop star, you have to accept that the media are going to be your bedfellows for as long as you have a successful career. Because when they stop 'papping', you'll know it's all over.

Every emerging artist needs as much promotion as he or she can get; you're unlikely to become famous without the interest of the media.

The job of the press is to produce informative, interesting and entertaining stories. The relationship becomes mutually beneficial if an artist or their manager provides the media with such stories. Of course, you can spend an hour talking to the press about how brilliant your band is, and then make a single negative comment about anything, and you can be assured that that will be the headline the next day. In fact, you'll find yourself courted by the press if you're prone to controversial statements or issuing barbed soundbites about other artists.

Think back to the halcyon days of Britpop and the acres of tabloid headlines spawned by the 'rivalry' between Oasis and Blur. It generated the kind of hype that had the record companies cracking open the champagne bottles.

The problems start when stars achieve a level of success and think that they can turn off the media, the hype and the headlines. Whereas once they courted publicity, suddenly they find the media an inconvenience and they bellyache about 'intrusion'. It doesn't work that way. Celebrities make a pact with the devil and they have to live with that. Successful artists look at the perks of the job and realize that they are well compensated for their loss of privacy.

The truth is that if an artist really doesn't want to be 'papped', he or she doesn't have to be. Many famous stars have had little problem staying out of the limelight. Ask Kate Bush. Or Larry Mullen of U2. While Bono is omnipresent in the media, the only time you see Larry Mullen is when the band is on tour.

If stars insist on wining and dining at 'celebrity' restaurants and falling out of clubs at all hours of the morning, they become easy prey. The paparazzi wait for celebrities to pour out of these haunts and hope that they can capture anyone making a fool of themselves. There's also the added problem that celebrities get too much free drink in clubs, attract the wrong kind of attention, and things can get horribly out of control.

Just ask Cheryl from Girls Aloud. She was found guilty of assaulting a toilet attendant, but thankfully was cleared of racially aggravated assault. It was an ordeal that could have ended her career.

THE PRESS RELEASE

The truth is that the media welcomes any interesting story with open arms. If you provide a story, you will get your headline.

▶ Cheryl from Girls Aloud attracted the kind of publicity that might have ended her career.

Want to publicize your new demo or a gig that you're performing? Or perhaps you want to create a little media 'buzz' about yourself or your band? Send out a press release. See P for Press Pack.

Unfortunately, many artists and managers feel that their new single or gig is news in itself. Yet 'Singer Does Gig' and 'Singer Releases Single' are not the kind of headlines you see in your average newspaper or magazine. So the best you can hope for is that news of your gig may make it into the entertainment or event listings carried in newspapers and on local radio stations.

It's even more likely that your press release will end up in some journalist's bin if you don't take the trouble to find the name of the actual individual who assembles these listings. Call your local newspapers and radio stations and get the name and contact details of that person, then send your press release to him or her personally. That said, if you want to generate a buzz about yourself, it's going to take more than just appearing in the listings.

MAKING HEADLINES

Making the headlines requires constant creative thinking and hype.

When Boyzone were in Australia during the early part of their career, they hit a bit of turbulence on an internal flight. I told a few journalists that they had crash-landed in the outback and it made the front page of several newspapers. The press were happy and the band got publicity; the only problem was that I forgot to warn the guys' families, who were shocked at the headlines about how their sons had nearly died. OK, it was a huge exaggeration based on a little kernel of fact, because the lads really did think they were going to crash.

I certainly don't recommend lying, because lies will be uncovered. In this case I knew I wasn't going to get caught out because Australia really was far away in those days. Now, of course, the internet spreads news like wildfire and my 'hype' would have been uncovered immediately.

Here are some ideas to start you thinking about how to create your own headlines.

FAST TRACK TIPS TO MAKING HEADLINES

Piggyback on a Celebrity

Date a famous footballer. It didn't do Cheryl Cole from Girls Aloud any harm. Or an actor. Nadine Coyle from Girls Aloud made the headlines when she started dating Jesse Metcalfe from *Desperate Housewives*. And there were lots more headlines when they broke up. Nicky Byrne also generated a great deal of press when Westlife were formed, because he was already dating the Irish prime minister's daughter, Georgina Ahern.

It's also great if you can tell the press truthfully that you are Cliff Richard's distant cousin or Sting's niece or nephew. It's even better if you can get one of these celebrities to endorse your career and give you a quote for your press release.

If you haven't got a celebrity in your life, go out and get one. Many artists are happy to sign autographs at the backstage door after gigs or shows. Tell them you're a budding star and they'll no doubt wish you good luck. Then you can legitimately send out a press release and photo saying 'U2 star Bono Gives Thumbs Up to New Singer'. The rest of the press release can detail your delight at meeting Bono and how he wished you luck when you told him about your career ambitions.

Human Interest Angle

Come up with a good human interest angle. Do you have a day job that contrasts dramatically with your music career ambitions? There's a *Fame*-style movie from the eighties called *Flashdance*, starring Jennifer Beals. She plays a grubby welder who desperately wants to go to ballet school. The movie wouldn't have been very gripping if Jennifer had played a make-up artist trying to go to ballet school, now would it?

Struggling against the odds can also make for a good story. Maybe you have overcome some major trauma or incident and you're bouncing back, determined to become a star.

Exploit Glamour

It may be sexist, but all newspapers love beautiful girls. If you have a great photo to go with your press release, the papers will find some excuse to use it. It's even better if your press release tells how you sacrificed a modelling career for your music. However, this story is not going to be very convincing if the accompanying photograph shows someone who is four stone overweight.

Fast Track TV Fame

Kylie, Jason and Delta Goodrem kicked off their music careers on the back of the TV soap *Neighbours*. It was easy for them to attract the media. Other ambitious wannabe pop stars can now do the same with so many reality TV show opportunities out there. The Ordinary Boys were rather ordinary until Samuel Preston appeared on *Celebrity Big Brother*.

An appearance on ordinary *Big Brother* or any other TV show is a big help for an emerging artist or band. See J for Jobs for details of sites that advertise castings for these TV programmes. You'll need to get your video camera out and record a killer showreel, and you'll need to make an impact within seconds before the casting director cries 'Next!'

Generate Controversy

Amy Winehouse made headlines when she heckled Bono at the Q Awards in 2006, while Jarvis Cocker's stage invasion during Michael Jackson's performance at the 1996 Brit Awards has gone down in the pop annals. Sinéad O'Connor will never be forgotten for ripping up that photo of the Pope on American TV; actress Liz Hurley's career was born when she appeared in a dress held together by safety pins. I could go on and on . . .

FAST TRACK TO CONTACTING THE MEDIA

Take a look at the International Showcase Music Book, which is online at www.showcase-music.com. Copies may also be available in your local library.

A listing of local, regional and national press, radio and TV in the UK and Northern Ireland is also available on www.nusonline.co.uk.

In Ireland, the Broadcasting Commission of Ireland has local, regional and national radio and TV stations in their list of licensed operators. See www.bci.ie.

You'll find free contact details for all Irish media, including newspapers, magazines, radio and TV at www.medialive.ie.

The definitive guide in Ireland is the Irish Media Contacts Directory, which costs €100 for a twelve-month subscription and two editions published in May and November. It's published by Media Contact; see www.mediacontact.ie; phone (01) 473 2050.

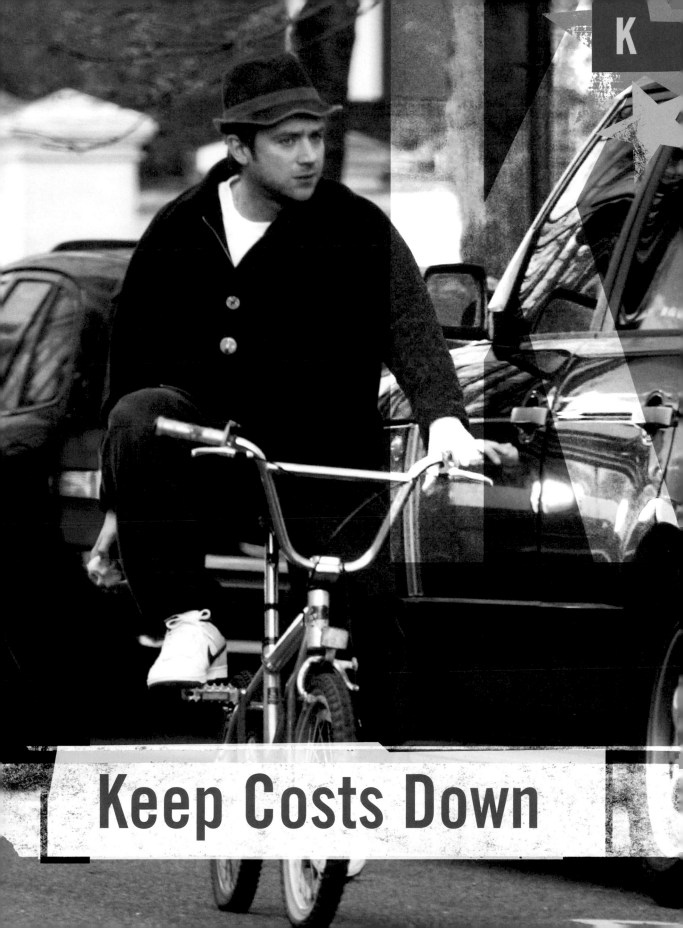

K

Keep Costs Down

KEEP COSTS DOWN
MONEY FOR NOTHING!

MONEY WAS DEFINITELY too tight to mention when Boyzone started out. We encountered all sorts of financial problems – once the band even had to flee a London hotel when they couldn't pay the bill. This was before they ever

launched a single in the UK. They were in London to record the Osmonds' track 'Love Me For A Reason', which later became their first hit. They should have had enough money to pay for the hotel, but one of the guys sent the bill through the roof by spending hours on the hotel phone. And unfortunately he wasn't calling his dear old mother back in Ireland; he had spent his time calling phone sex lines at premium rates.

I'll spare his blushes by not naming the culprit, but needless to say the guys had a heart attack when they saw the size of the bill the next morning.

'I think the bill was for around six hundred pounds, which was a hell of a lot of money at the time,' recalls Keith Duffy. 'I don't think one person can take the blame because we were all using the phone. But desperate times call for desperate measures so we decided to leg it. I think it was The President Hotel we were in, but it was a very amateur escape. First of all Ronan and Shane went out the fire escape and set off the hotel alarm. The hotel was located over a bank and here we were throwing these cases out the window into the street with all these people watching inside the bank. And then the other three of us sauntered through reception, got outside, and then all five of us were legging it down a busy London street. We heard all these police sirens and, God love us, we were so innocent – we thought the cops were combing the streets of London for us.'

The lads knew I'd hit the roof, so they were cute enough not to tell me about their great escape until much later. Here was I and their co-manager, John Reynolds, desperately trying to market them as wholesome Irish boy-next-door types. Conning a hotel out of a payment for premium rate phone sex lines was not exactly the kind of press we were looking for at the time.

FAST TRACK TIP TO MONEY FOR NOTHING

Check out the Fundersonline.org website, which has a guide to funding research and how to apply for funding. It has good links and lists of sources of funding. See www. fundersonline.org/grantseekers.

FINDING FINANCIAL HELP

When you're starting out as a music artist, you'll know all about being broke. However, fleeing hotels or other premises without paying your bill is definitely not recommended.

Banks don't tend to lend money to those who really need it, but there are thousands of organizations out there providing free money in the form of grants, bursaries and sponsorships. Budding stars can get valuable training, musical instruments and access to recording studios with the right grants. The big problem about getting your hands on funding is that it involves hard work and is very time consuming. However, it's an investment well worth making if it helps you succeed in the music business.

Applying for funding is a real skill, and an estimated 90 per cent of applications for funding are declined. This is due to a lack of research and understanding of the organization and how it awards funds. However, if you do your research properly, you may find what Dire Straits referred to as 'Money for Nothing'!

Me and Stephen Gately of Boyzone, who knew all about money problems when we were starting out.

FAST TRACK TO MUSIC GRANTS

Here are a few of the organizations who may be sympathetic to requests for funding or training from singers, bands and music artists.

The Arts Council

The Arts Council offers grants to individuals of £200 to £30,000; their average grant is £5,580. The Northern Ireland branch has made available grants of up to £5,000 for bands who need musical instruments, while the Irish Arts Council gives bursaries and training awards to young musicians.

Arts Council of England:
see **www.artscouncil.org.uk**;
phone **0845 300 6200**.
Arts Council of Scotland:
see **www.scottisharts.org.uk**;
phone **0845 603 6000**.Arts Council of Wales: see **www.arts wales.org.uk**;
phone **(029) 237 6500**.
Arts Council of Northern Ireland:
see **www.artscouncil-ni.org**;
phone **(028) 9038 5200**.
Arts Council of Ireland:
see **www.artscouncil.ie**;
phone **(01) 618 0200**.

The Prince's Trust

Are you struggling in school? Have you been in care? Have you been in trouble with the law? Are you long-term unemployed? If you are aged between fourteen and thirty and answered yes to any of these questions, then you have a chance of applying for a grant of between £50 and £500 for training courses. The Trust also offers Sound Live and Dance Live courses. These are six-day residential courses in music or dance, which are free to eighteen to twenty-five year olds with a basic knowledge of a musical instrument or the use of decks. Accommodation, food and transport are included. See **www.princes-trust.org.uk**; freephone **0800 842 842**.

Me with my pal Prince Charles who runs The Prince's Trust.

Youth Music

Youth Music is a UK-wide charity set up in 1999 to provide high-quality and diverse music-making opportunities for individuals aged up to eighteen. However, it only funds organizations rather than individuals. If you are a music maker and have an idea for a programme or project, you can approach an organization and ask it to agree to be the main applicant. See **www.youthmusic.org.uk**.

The British Record Industry Trust

The Brit Trust funds the only non-fee-paying performing arts school in the UK. The Brit School in Croydon, South London is a full-time state school for fourteen to nineteen year olds, and is dedicated to training in the arts and media. Former pupils include recording star Katie Melua and Leona Lewis who was the *X Factor* winner in 2006. See **www.brittrust.co.uk**; phone **(020) 7803 1300**.

PRS Foundation for New Music

This adventurous body funds original music in all genres, including pop and rock. Its funding ranges from £500 to £15,000, but the average grant is £4,000. They don't give grants to individuals or for college fees or equipment purchase, but they have funded many bands and helped them to tour, perform live and distribute CDs, etc. See **www.prsfoundation.co.uk**; phone **(020) 7306 4044**.

EMI Music Sound Foundation

This independent music education charity aims to improve young people's access to music education in the UK and Ireland. They are the single largest sponsor of specialist performing arts colleges and have created vital bursaries at seven music colleges to assist students in need of financial support. See **www.emimusicsoundfoundation.com**; phone **(020) 7795 7000**.

Women in Music

This organization celebrates women's music making across all genres. They award grants and provide 'mentoring' schemes to support female musicians. See **www.womeninmusic.org.uk**.

IMRO (Irish Music Rights Organization)

IMRO runs the Bill Whelan International Music Bursary to help gifted music students attend third level institutes overseas. See **www.imro.ie**; phone **(01) 661 4844**.

IRMA (Irish Recorded Music Association)

The IRMA Trust is a non-profit charity that works with young people who wish to pursue a career in music. It has an instrument lending library, providing musical instruments to organizations and individuals. It has also funded rehearsal studios for musicians aged twelve to twenty-six in Limerick and Kerry. See **www.irmatrust.ie**; phone **(01) 284 5505**.

Lawyers
Live Performing

LAWYERS
SIGN ON THE DOTTED LINE

NINE INCH NAILS star Trent Reznor went to court after learning that, instead of having millions, he had just $400,000 (£204,000) in cash. He sued his manager, claiming that he had been duped into signing a bad contract. However, he admitted that he'd ignored his finances and carelessly signed documents without understanding them. He still won his case in 2005 and was awarded $3 million (£1.53 million).

Legendary singer-songwriter Leonard Cohen claimed he was left with just $150,000 (£76,000) in his retirement fund after he was defrauded of $5 million (£2.6 million) by Kelley Lynch, his ex-manager. Lynch didn't respond to a civil case law suit initiated by Cohen and, in 2005, claimed that her phone had been disconnected as she didn't have the money to pay her bill. So it is unlikely that Cohen will recover the $9.5 million (£4.85 million) that the court awarded him in 2006.

Yes, artists can be swindled out of their earnings, but not if they're careful. If you're serious about a music career, you need a good music lawyer and accountant as soon as you're presented with a contract. It's tempting to sign the first contract that's put in front of you because you're so desperate to break into the industry. However, make a bad deal and you can pay for it for your entire career. The music lawyer is extremely important because a single line in a contract can mean the difference between riches and living on the breadline.

Top music lawyers charge by the hour, but they can recoup their costs many times over as soon as they start poring over a contract. You can go to the Musicians' Union for legal advice, which is usually free. See U for Unions. However, you are really expected to seek independent legal advice before you sign a record or publishing deal. In fact you'd be silly not to. An expert music lawyer dealing with successful acts will also have many contacts in the business that can be used to your advantage.

HOW MUCH WILL A MUSIC LAWYER COST?

Hourly rates in the UK range from £250 to £350 per hour. It will cost more if you have to take or defend an action – litigation lawyers cost £500 upwards.

FAST TRACK GUIDE TO FINDING A MUSIC LAWYER

The International Association of Entertainment Lawyers has over 200 members in twenty countries around the world. Their website allows you to search and find entertainment lawyers, and gives all contact details, including websites, if applicable. See www.iael.org.

> *When two dogs fight over a bone and a third runs off with it, that's the lawyer.*
>
> German proverb

▶ Nine Inch Nails star Trent Reznor should have taken the advice of a good lawyer.

FAST TRACK TIP ON 'LAWYERS'

Legal professionals are usually referred to as solicitors in this part of the world. However, those who work in the music business are known as 'lawyers', just like their American counterparts. So never talk about getting a solicitor to look over your contract or you will catch the music pros exchanging amused glances and shaking their world-weary heads.

LIVE PERFORMING
GET OFF THE STAGE

When you walk out in front of 300,000 people and pull it off, it validates you.

Sheryl Crow

IF ANYONE WAS going to mess up a live Boyzone performance, it was Keith Duffy. 'We were in Manchester,' he recalls. 'We had an audience of eighteen thousand and it was also going out on pay-per-view TV so it was massive. At one stage we were meant to sit on steps in a V formation at the back of the stage. Instead I strolled out to the front of the stage and realized that there was no one behind me. I didn't want to mess up so I tried to make it all look intentional. I sat down Red Indian style at the front of the stage and tried to act natural. I might have got away with it too if the others hadn't started p***ing themselves laughing!'

X Factor's Shayne Ward also realized very early on that no matter how long you rehearse, things still go wrong. During one of his first shows in Dublin in January 2007, he was abseiling from the ceiling of the Point when the lowering mechanism jammed halfway. As the crew desperately tried to fix the machine, Shayne hung there, trying to pretend this mid-air break was part of the show.

Murphy's Law dictates that if a live performance can go wrong, it will. U2 were trapped in their giant lemon pod on the Pop Mart Tour in Norway, and I've lost count of the times Westlife have been left hanging by harnesses from the ceilings of arenas.

Westlife's Brian McFadden became a stand-up comic when the backing music failed. Real professionals are never thrown by a stage catastrophe and Spinal Tap moments. They just keep doing what they're supposed to do – entertaining the audience.

Equipment will blow up, microphones will break down, backing tracks will start skipping; always have a back-up plan – it's an important part of earning a reputation as a professional performer.

WHY PERFORM LIVE?

To Improve Your Performance and Material

One of the best ways of developing your performance skills is to perform live.

To Promote Your Performance

Performing live is a great way of generating a fan base, showcasing your talents and promoting yourself as a performer. A record company is unlikely to sign you without a proven ability to perform live and promote your records. Live gigs also help develop your own buzz in the music press.

To Earn a Living

Yes, it's true that the record business has been in a decline as a result of illegal downloading. However, ticket sales for live music acts are up 25 per cent in recent years. Artists are making more money than ever – they're just not making as much of it from record sales, so the ability to perform live is vital for the health of your bank balance.

DO I NEED PERMISSION TO PERFORM COVER VERSIONS OF SONGS?

No. The venue must have a PRS (Performing Right Society) licence that enables you to perform live music and cover songs. So-called 'significant venues' even have to provide lists of the songs. For more details on the PRS see C for Collection Societies, C for Copyright and R for Royalties.

HOW MUCH DO I GET PAID FOR LIVE PERFORMANCES?

How long is a piece of string? It depends on the venue, the audience size and your act. However, the Musicians' Union issues general gig rate guidelines. They suggest acts should be paid a minimum of £56.50 for engagements of up to two hours, or £68 for up to three hours in pubs and clubs before midnight. After midnight the rate rises.

They suggest a casual stage rate in theatre and concert venues of £115 for performances of up to three hours, or £104 for venues with a capacity of 300 or less. These are absolute minimum rates – you are free to negotiate a much better deal. See U for Unions for more details.

FAST TRACK IDEAS TO PERFORMING LIVE

★ Solo pop acts or groups don't need a band to perform live. All they need are backing tracks and a PA system (see below). See B for Backing Tracks.

★ Get listed for free with the annual entertainment guide, *The White Book*, at **www.whitebook.co.uk**; phone **(024) 7657 1176**. This is used by event planners to

source everything from musicians to marquees. Also sign up with musician-finder websites such as **www.partysounds.co.uk**, which is a free band directory for the UK and Northern Ireland. For weddings, get listed on sites such as **www. weddings.co.uk**, **www.weddingsonline.ie** and **www.irishweddingsonline.com**. There are also sister sites for Welsh, Ulster and Scottish weddings. The Musicians' Union keeps a region-by-region record of acts for anyone interested. And check out the entertainment directory at **www.entsweb.co.uk**; a standard entry costs £10.

★ The best way to get live gigs is through an agent who has established contacts with venues and will promote you. The problem is that many music agents will only take on signed acts. Entertainment agents will work with unsigned artists for parties and weddings, etc., but only if you have experience of performing live. See A for Agents.

★ You may not need an agent for smaller clubs and pubs. Approach local venues yourself with your demo and press pack.

★ Hire your own venue or function room in a pub and stage a show for your friends and family. Improve your chances of filling the venue by teaming up with other bands or DJs, and make a big night of it.

★ If you're already performing in your local area, why not exchange gigs with another band? Find an act that is performing live in the next town, persuade them to put you on their bill as a support act, and then return the favour for them.

★ There are hundreds of festivals all around the UK and Ireland, and many smaller ones may welcome a performer volunteering to fill a spot. Some even pay a basic fee. Don't get too ambitious: you're dreaming if you think an unsigned artist can appear at Glastonbury.

★ Check out J for Jobs for other sites and publications that advertise live performance opportunities, such as cruise ships, clubs, holiday camps, etc. Check the small ads of papers like *Loot* or music magazines for anyone looking for bands, singers and musicians.

THE PA SYSTEM

The PA system is an amplifier and loudspeaker system that allows the audience to hear you. Of course, if you're performing acoustically in an intimate setting, you may not need any amplification. However, in most public settings you will require it. Bigger music venues will often have in-house systems, but smaller clubs, pubs or restaurants may expect you to provide your own.

A PA system is expensive, but you can also hire one until such time as you are performing live regularly and can afford your own. Talk to other performers, try out different models, research the right system and check out what's available second-hand before you think of blowing the budget.

MAKING THE MOST OF YOUR LIVE PERFORMANCES

★ Always do a sound check before a gig so there's no tuning up or preparation needed when you get on stage. As soon as you appear before an audience, you should be 'on', not 'coming on'.

★ There's no point in performing a great show and letting people walk away without knowing your name. Don't hide your light under a bushel. Make sure there is a backdrop or banner emblazoned with your name.

★ Don't be the only one who doesn't see the gig. Tape your performance and review it later. U2 still tape their concerts to see how they can improve their performance. Learn from the masters.

★ Be prepared. Have your press or promotional pack ready to hand over to anyone who registers a professional interest.

★ Sell your own CDs and merchandise at every gig.

★ Even if only a handful of people turn up for your gig, play your heart out. Make it a private party to remember.

★ Appoint one person to collect the money at every gig. If there are any payment problems, it's always useful to have the Musicians' Union on your side. See U for Unions.

▶ Kaiser Chiefs make the most of their live performance with a banner backdrop.

129 ★

Managers
Merchandise

MANAGERS
THE MAIN MAN

> I knew what I was looking at. It was sex.
> And I was just ahead of the pack.
>
> Manager Andrew Oldham, who discovered
> the Rolling Stones

THE ROAD TO fame is littered with the wasted careers of artists who refused to listen to their managers. The Monkees were doing great until they decided they wanted to be a 'credible' act and write their own material. The resulting album, *Headquarters*, was a disaster. Don Kirshner, the band's manager and mastermind, became fed up and resigned. He gave his next great pop song, 'Sugar Sugar', to the animated characters The Archies. He said he wanted a band that didn't talk back. That was the end of The Monkees.

America's biggest ever boyband, New Kids on the Block, did the same. They decided they didn't need their manager, Maurice Starr. They gave themselves an image makeover and returned with a new tough, street look. They bombed. End of career.

Ronan Keating's solo career was doing very nicely until he also decided he wanted 'credibility'. He dumped me and brought out a rock album, *Turn it On*. It was a massive flop. However, he went back to doing what his audience loves best – ballads – and no doubt he'll still have a long career ahead of him.

The moral of this tale is that **there's no point in having a manager if you're not willing to be managed.**

WHAT DOES A MANAGER DO?

A good manager is the hub in a big wheel of agents, promoters, record companies, publishers, press, producers, accountants and lawyers. He or she deals with all aspects of an artist's career, from publicity and tours to song selection and record deals. A really successful manager is multi-skilled, multi-tasking and involved in both the creative and business side of an artist's career.

The most important job for a manager is to secure a record deal and publishing contract for his or her artists. They then look after the business side of things to ensure the artists make money. A good manager should also be involved in the creative process and help define the artist's sound and image, finding the right producers to work on the songs and ensuring the artists get the hits they want.

They may run the business, but a manager never has control of an artist's bank account; every artist should sign their own cheques.

WHEN DO YOU GET A MANAGER?

Ronan Keating fired me.

You need a manager when you've done as much as you can by yourself. Have you recorded a good-quality demo? Are you performing live or do you feel ready to perform live? Have you been offered a record deal? If you've answered 'yes' to more than one of these questions, it's time to look for a manager.

Some artists are capable of managing themselves, but not many do this successfully. Having said that, it's better that you manage yourself than end up with the wrong manager. Choose carefully, as the right manager can make a huge impact on your career, while the wrong man/woman can effectively hobble the career of even the most talented artist. If you can't find the right person for you, do without one until you can.

FAST TRACK TO FINDING A MANAGER

Close to Home

Some artists do not stray far from home when looking for their manager. Beyoncé has done very well using her dad as her manager, while Britney Spears, Delta Goodrem and Jewel launched very successful careers with the help of their mums. But, it's unusual to have a parent who has enough showbiz savvy to manage an artist successfully.

Established Manager

A manager who has already had success in your chosen music field can provide a fast track route to fame. After my success with Boyzone, it was much easier securing a record deal for my second boyband, Westlife. Unfortunately, managers who are already successful are usually too busy to take on new artists.

Word of Mouth

Finding the right manager involves research. Talk to other artists and musicians and see who they recommend. If you have a music lawyer, accountant or agent, talk to them and ask for recommendations.

 Coldplay were managed by a college pal.

Enthusiastic Novice

Sometimes you don't need a manager with a proven track record. Inexperienced Paul McGuinness made an international success out of U2 because he was just as passionate about their music as they were. And Coldplay were propelled to rock fame by a friend who studied at Oxford – Phil Harvey. He was simply enthusiastic, bright and loved their music.

Let the Manager Come to You

One of the best ways to find a manager is to make yourself such an attractive proposition that they come looking for you. If you've released your own record or built up an appreciative audience through live gigging, they'll come flocking.

For more suggestions and a checklist to help you find the perfect manager, go to **www.musicmanagersforum.co.uk**.

MANAGERS

HOW MUCH DOES A MANAGER GET PAID?

If anyone asks you for money upfront, they are not a real manager. See H for The HoaX Factor.

Elvis's manager, Colonel Tom Parker, took 50 per cent; the Beatles' Brian Epstein is said to have taken 25 per cent. I like the nice round figure of 20 per cent of gross earnings, which is more realistic today. This means the manager gets paid 20 per cent of an artist's income before expenses are deducted. However, managers usually agree to take 20 per cent of net income on live performing (after expenses), because there are so many costs involved. See C for Concerts. Of course, you can try to negotiate a lower percentage, but be warned: a manager with a good track record is unlikely to accept a lower rate of commission.

HOW LONG IS A MANAGEMENT CONTRACT?

Never sign a long-term management contract until you are absolutely sure that you can work with this person. Suggest a three-month trial period for both parties and see how you get on. The typical term of a management contract is between three and five years.

There are usually get-out clauses that will allow both parties to end the contract after twelve months. Do remember, though, that even if you and your manager part company, they will still earn commission on records produced during the term of the contract. This post-term commission can last up to ten years.

FAST TRACK TIP ON MANAGERS

There are three types of manager: the control freak who keeps his or her artists on a short leash; the 'Yes' manager who does everything to please the artist so that they can hold on to their job; and the money-grubbing manager who is only interested in the $$$. I like to think that the really successful manager is a blend of all three – like me.

FAST TRACK TO THE GREAT MANAGERS

Simon Fuller

Simon Fuller of 19 Entertainment managed the Spice Girls and created the TV talent shows *Pop Idol* and *American Idol*.

Tom Watkins

Tom Watkins is retired now, but used to manage Bros, East 17 and The Pet Shop Boys.

Nigel Martin Smith

The genius behind Take That, Nigel Martin Smith now runs the Nemesis casting and model agency in Manchester.

Andy Stevens
The long-time manager of George Michael.

Roger Davies
A former Australian roadie, Roger Davies managed Janet Jackson and Tina Turner, and currently has Cher, Sade, Pink and Joe Cocker on his books.

Benny Medina
The American behind the success of J Lo, Mariah Carey and Brandy.

Billy Sammeth
Billy Sammeth was hired and fired a total of twenty-three times by Cher. He also steered stars such as the Osmonds and Olivia Newton-John to fame, and was a panellist on the TV hit *Soapstar Superstar*.

Nicky Ryan
The manager and creator of the globally successful Enya brand. Enya is not so much an individual as a registered trademark owned by Nicky, who is also a producer, his wife Roma, who writes the lyrics, and Eithne Ní Bhraonáin, who sings and writes the music.

Sharon Osbourne
Housewife superstar and canny rock manager, Sharon Osbourne masterminded Ozzy's success. She also worked with Motörhead, ELO and Gary Moore.

Paul McGuinness
He is the loyal and extremely hard-working manager of Ireland's most successful music act ever, U2, and much of the drive and vision behind one of the world's most successful and enduring rock bands.

Irving Azoff
Irving Azoff has managed Steely Dan and The Eagles for ever, and now works with Christina Aguilera, Jewel, Seal and Van Halen. He has a reputation as a very loyal and tough manager.

John Reid
This Scotsman found unknown Reginald Dwight and turned him into superstar Elton John. He remained Elton's manager for twenty-eight years, before they had a major legal battle over money. He has also worked with Queen, Kiki Dee, Barry Humphries, Billy Connolly, Michael Flatley, and managed the Jackson Five when Michael was just eleven.

Brian Epstein
The late, great genius behind the Beatles, Gerry and the Pacemakers and Cilla Black.

Peter Grant
The late, great manager of Led Zeppelin and The Yardbirds.

MERCHANDISE
HOW MUCH IS THAT T-SHIRT IN THE WINDOW?

I felt a bit bad ordering changes, but hey, it's my doll!

Britney Spears

THE BRITNEY SPEARS doll became the biggest-selling celebrity doll ever issued, so it looks as though she was right to insist on changes.

The demand for merchandise at Boyzone's early shows took us by surprise. At one of their first shows, every single branded item – photos, posters, programmes, T-shirts, key rings – sold out in fifty minutes. Our astonished merchandiser David Bell – who runs Seminal Merchandising in Dublin – remarked that Boyzone fans would buy anything. For a laugh he took off a shoe, wrote Boyzone on the side, and put it on the concession stand beside us. Within seconds a fan had pounced on the shoe; it wasn't easy persuading a little girl that it was all just a joke.

And it's not always easy being a merchandiser. Boyzone's Stephen Gately spent a day pedalling a pushbike furiously around Wembley Arena in hot pursuit of David. He had seen his new photo on sale in the arena and he wasn't happy with it. Ideally, all merchandise should be approved by the band. However, it's a nightmare getting every single member of the band together to agree to everything. I probably signed off on it and blamed David. Of course, in the end Stephen's photo turned out to be the biggest seller of the five Boyzone shots.

WHAT IS MERCHANDISE?

If you've ever bought a poster, photograph, T-shirt, key ring or pen with your favourite band's name or logo on it, you've bought merchandise.

My good friend Sharon Osbourne and her husband, Ozzy, saw merchandise sales rocket as a result of the success of their MTV show, *The Osbournes*. Ozzy even set a record for heavy metal artists, as **sales of 'Ozzy for President' T-shirts, mugs and action figures soared to £27 million during the height of Osbourne mania.**

Successful pop acts can also expect to make millions from their official merchandise; for many artists it's a more lucrative source of income than record sales.

137 ★

FAST TRACK TO EARNINGS FROM MERCHANDISE

The Advance

Rival merchandising companies bid to manufacture and sell the merchandise of successful acts. This normally involves the offer of an advance on merchandising royalties, which may be £50,000 for an up-and-coming band, and millions of pounds for a megastar act such as U2 (see below).

Acts with Older Audiences

Older audiences attracted to cool indie bands or acts such as Coldplay tend to spend very little on posters, badges and key rings. The average taking is around £2–3 per head. Only superstar acts with older audiences such as Bruce Springsteen and U2 will command £4–5 per head. U2 are unique in that they can double that take in America.

Over 80 per cent of sales in this age group are related to T-shirts and other clothing.

Acts with Younger Audiences

Pop acts such as McFly, Justin Timberlake and Kylie, who attract younger audiences, tend to make more per head in merchandising – at least £5–6 per person on top of the ticket price. That's because younger fans are much more likely to splash out on the T-shirts, key rings and posters of their pop idols.

I hear Take That's reunion tour beat the merchandising sales of most other pop and rock acts, with whopping takings of £6–7 per head.

Over 80 per cent of sales in this age group are related to paper products such as posters and programmes.

The Material Girl's merchandise expanded in 2007 when she launched her own fashion collection called M by Madonna for H&M.

Top of the Merchandise Pops

Forget a career in music and train as a wrestler. Beating most pop and rock acts hands down in the merchandise stakes is the WWF (World Wrestling Federation), which earns a massive £15 per head in branded goods. Disney actress-turned-singer Hilary Duff also stunned merchandisers with average sales of £10–12 per head during her first UK tour in 2006.

MERCHANDISE OUTGOINGS

Before artists see a penny of the merchandising income, 25 per cent goes to the venue in which the products were sold. This percentage is considerably higher in the US.

HOW MUCH DOES THE ARTIST MAKE?

The artist takes 45 per cent or more of the merchandising income after the owner of the venue has received his share, and after the revenue commissioners have been paid. If a T-shirt is priced at £20, the artist's share is around £7. That's great news if you're a solo artist like Shayne Ward, but Girls Aloud split that £7 between five, resulting in income of £1.40 each.

Artists such as Madonna, who charge huge amounts for merchandise, command an even larger percentage. Some collect 100 per cent of the profit and pay the merchandisers a flat fee to sell the product.

MERCHANDISING TROUBLE

Of course, if a tour is cancelled or the merchandisers don't make back their advance, they have the right to a refund. This is not the same as a record deal, where the advance is recoupable but not refundable; an advance on merchandising royalties is both recoupable and refundable.

The members of pop band S Club 7 were actually sued by their merchandising company after three members of the band were caught in possession of cannabis. The group faced an £800,000 lawsuit from PMS International in 2002, who claimed that the group's drugs scandal the year before had ruined sales. It emerged that PMS had bought the worldwide rights to make official S Club 7 items, including toys, stationery, lunch boxes, mugs, make-up sets and bags, for £630,000.

BOOTLEGS

Pirated T-shirts and bootleg merchandising is a constant headache and a drain on an artist's income. However, official merchandisers can use your trademarked name and logo to sue anyone infringing their copyright or illegally producing merchandise in an artist's name.

U2 breaks the merchandising mould in the US. They are such an iconic act in America that they can earn nearly double the £4–5 per head average spent on branded material.

U2 performed before 4.6 million fans on their last tour, 'Vertigo', which wrapped up in December 2006. So you can understand why merchandising companies would fall over each other trying to bid for the rights to make and sell their merchandise. I've heard on the grapevine that the band received an advance on merchandising royalties of between £10 and £15 million on 'Vertigo'.

In fact, U2 own a big share of the merchandising company, De-Lux, which makes most of their branded products. So the band not only receive their advance, but a share of the merchandising company's profits too.

De-Lux also looks after the merchandise for acts such as Justin Timberlake, George Michael, J Lo, Madonna, Scissor Sisters, Kylie Minogue, Gnarls Barkley, Coldplay, Aerosmith, Kanye West, Britney Spears, Maroon Five, Alicia Keys, Bjork and The Feeling – the list goes on and on. So U2 are also making money from the merchandise sales of many of the biggest artists in the world.

U2 are not just pretty faces, are they?

FAST TRACK TO DIY MERCHANDISING

If you're not signed to a record label, you're not going to get a merchandising deal. But there's nothing to stop you getting your own T-shirts, singles, badges and general promotional material manufactured and selling them on your own website.

You don't even have to have your own website to sell your merchandise. Internet shops such as **www.cafepress.com** give you your own shop front and do all the manufacturing and shipping of T-shirts, CDs, badges, etc. in exchange for a percentage of products sold. They set the base price for each item and you can increase it to whatever amount you want your fans to pay for each item. A customized T-shirt featuring your name, logo and photo can cost less than £5 on cafepress.com. You can also order at cost price in bulk and sell them at your live performances. This company is based in the US but accepts orders internationally. You can tell people via your MySpace site how they can buy your merchandise, or you can use giveaways for promotional purposes. See **www.cafepress.com**.

Many local printers and companies supply similar services, so check **www.yell.com** in the UK or **www.goldenpages.ie** in Ireland, then start comparing prices.

Naming Your Act

Niceness

NAMING YOUR ACT
THE TITLE PAGE

MOST OF YOU will be familiar with the name 'Westlife'. Well, for quite some time they were called Westside.

The biggest teething trouble with this band was naming them. In the very beginning, the guys came to me as I.O.U. However, no one liked the name, and Simon Cowell wanted it changed as soon as the band was signed to his label. We wanted a name that reflected their West of Ireland origins. Then one day I was driving through Ranelagh, a suburb of Dublin, and I saw the name 'Westside' on a yellow skip. So that's what they became.

Then, just as we were about to release Westside's début single, we discovered we had a major problem. The name was registered and being used by a rap band in America. It was a disaster as the band had already toured Ireland and the UK on a really successful *Smash Hits* Roadshow and as the support act on Boyzone's tour. All the merchandise was branded 'Westside'.

Nevertheless, the label insisted that there was no alternative but to change the name again. We had to find something nearly identical to Westside and we came up with Westlife. It was a case of third time lucky, because after doing various searches, it was confirmed the name belonged to no other act.

> *I buy it if I like the album cover. I buy it if I like the name of the band. I'll buy whatever catches my attention.*
> Bruce Springsteen

So their first single, 'Swear It Again', was released under the name Westlife. David Bell of Seminal Merchandising in Ireland is still kicking himself that he destroyed all the Westside posters and merchandise. He reckons he could have made himself a small fortune selling them as 'collectors' items' on eBay!

We had similar problems in the early days of Boyzone. The band had already released their first UK single when we discovered that there was a group in France already using the name. The French Boyzone were paid £15,000 – even though they had never recorded anything – so that we could use the name in France.

So it's worth doing all you can to avoid duplication of a band or artist's name. Mistakes lead to big financial and legal headaches further down the road. Obviously a record company will check this out for you when you get signed, but it's a lot of wasted effort if you have built up a following and then discover you can't in fact use the name. It makes sense to research your proposed name and then take steps to protect it.

FAST TRACK TO NAME-CALLING PROBLEMS

If someone else – a band, solo act or company – is already using the name you've chosen, they can take steps to prevent you from doing so, especially if they can prove they were using it first. It may seem bizarre, but even if you are a solo artist and plan to use your own name, you might not be able to if someone else is already performing under the same title.

Two bands using the same name in two different countries is no problem just as long as they stay in their separate countries. The trouble starts if one plans to tour or release records in the other country.

Who Owns the Name?

If a band splits up and the members go their separate ways, what happens to the name? If the band is signed, the record company usually owns the name. If not, the possession of the band's name should have been set out clearly in a formal band agreement (see B for Bands). Otherwise, no one has exclusive possession and the tug-of-war will either have to be resolved privately or in the courts.

FAST TRACK TO RESEARCHING AND PROTECTING YOUR NAME

The bad news is that you cannot copyright a band name, so it's not a straightforward legal process. However, there are steps you can take to ensure you have some legal protection.

[1] Undertake some simple research to see if anyone else is using your name. Google the name and search sites such as MySpace, Wikipedia and Amazon. Check to see if anyone has already registered the domain name on the internet by going to an easy domain search site such as **www.whois.com**. Remember to check .com sites as well as .org, .co.uk, .ie and .eu.

[2] Register your internet domain name, as you will definitely need your own website if you plan to be a success. This will also provide evidence that you were using this name from this date in case someone else starts using the name the following week. See I for Internet for tips.

[3] The online band registry, **www.bandname.com**, has no legal recognition. However, it is another useful means of checking whether someone has already laid claim to

the name. If they haven't, register your own act. This will provide evidence of when you began using the name, and may also reduce the problem of someone else choosing the same name at a later date. The site charges just £6.90 for a one-off registration.

[4] Register your band's name as a limited company, which will prevent anyone else using the same company name. You can also do a company search to see if your name is available.

The UK Companies Registration Office charges £20 to register a company name and £30 as a processing fee for the annual return. See **www.companieshouse.gov.uk**; phone **0870 333 3636**. The Irish Companies Registration Office charges €100 and a processing fee of €40 for the annual return. See **www.cro.ie**; lo-call (Ireland only) **1890 220226**.

[5] The most effective way to protect your band name is to register it as a trademark. The major problem with this is that it's expensive, as it has to be applied for separately in almost every country. And even if you trademark your band's music CDs, this will not protect your merchandise because that falls into another category and must be paid for independently. It's still a good idea to do an online trademark search to see if anyone else has already registered the name you want. If a company making ball bearings in Iowa shares your name, it's not too problematic; if it's another music act, you might want to consider a change.

The UK Patent Office charges £200 per trademark category. See **www.patent.gov.uk**; phone **(01633) 813930**. The Irish Patent Office charges €70 for an application and €177 for registration. Trademark lasts ten years. See **www.patentsoffice.ie**; lo-call (Ireland only) **1890 220223**. The US Patent & Trademark Office charges $325 per Federal trademark, which covers all states and lasts ten years. See **www.uspto.gov**; phone **(001) 571 272 1000**.

FAST TRACK TIP

If in doubt, check it out with a professional. This can be a complicated legal area, so if someone starts using your name and ignores a polite written request to stop, it's time to see a music lawyer. Similarly, if you receive a 'cease and desist' letter for using a name someone else is laying claim to, don't ignore it. Get legal advice.

DOUBLE TROUBLE

Popstars runners-up, Liberty X, lost a battle for their name when they discovered another group called Liberty existed before them. Still, it wasn't exactly a stretch to attach an 'X' to the name.

The boyband Blue also encountered legal problems when a Scottish rock act of the same name launched a high court case against them. And Blink 182 showed that by tacking on a few numbers to your name you can overcome the problem of discovering your first name choice is already taken.

Liberty had to be renamed Liberty X.

FAST TRACK TIP TO A SUCCESSFUL NAME

Research has shown that you're more likely to succeed if your act's name is longer than seven letters. And a sample of 2,000 American band names showed that bands whose names contained two words sold three times as many records as those with a single word. This doesn't always hold true – the brevity of U2's name hasn't hindered them!

FAST TRACK TO FINDING A NAME

Struggling to find an original name? Films have been a great source of inspiration for many bands. Black Sabbath is named after a 1963 horror movie starring Boris Karloff, while Duran Duran got its name from a villain in the 1968 movie *Barbarella*.

Some bands go for abbreviations, such as ABBA, which represents the initials of band members Agnetha, Björn, Benny and Anni-Frid.

Michael Stipe came up with the name REM (rapid eye movement) by sticking his finger in the dictionary. Others are inspired to name their bands by more prosaic means. The band Weezer was a school nickname for frontman Rivers Cuomo because he suffered from asthma.

Many solo artists have chosen to change their name. Cliff Richard was born Harry Webb; Engelbert Humperdinck's real name is Arnold Dorsey; Tom Jones is really Tom Woodward. One of my former acts, Johnny Logan, who won the Eurovision Song Contest three times, was born Sean Sherrard.

▶ Duran Duran got its name from a villain in the movie Barbarella starring Jane Fonda (below).

FAST TRACK TO FINDING A NAME VIRTUALLY

BANG (Band Automatic Name Generator)

This does exactly what it says on the label. Keep reloading the page and the names go on and on! There are an estimated 2 billion to choose from, and some of the suggestions I received were Perky Gravy, Silk Radius, Witless and Curly Spam. See **www.blamepro. com/bang.htm**.

Musicians' Friend Band and Song Name Generator

Go to the site map on the homepage as it's quite difficult to find otherwise. Look under the category 'Fun' and you'll see the 'Name Generator'. This one asks you to put in a single word and it comes up with endless variations. Go to **www.musiciansfriend.com**.

NICENESS
THE IMPORTANCE OF BEING EARNEST

> *I don't mean to be a diva, but some days you wake up and you're Barbra Streisand.*
>
> Courtney Love

FORMER WESTLIFE SINGER Brian McFadden tells a story about his first attempt to be a rock 'n' roll star. He was away from home, in a hotel room, and was feeling sorry for himself. So he drank the minibar and then tried to throw the TV out of the hotel window. It landed on his head.

When an artist starts behaving like a prat, everything tends to backfire. The UK and Ireland are small, word quickly gets around, people back off and a career starts unravelling. I'm not saying Brian is a prat, but he behaved like a prat on that day and can laugh at himself now.

I may be a manager, but don't call me if you have problems such as tantrums, homicidal rages, booze, pills or hookers. I don't work with people like that. I manage professionals, not egomaniacs, addicts or narcissists.

The guys from Boyzone were never as vocally talented as the guys from Westlife, and couldn't dance like the guys from Take That. Yet what they lacked in talent, they made up for in fun and charm. They always worked hard, they were ambitious, and people in the industry had a lot of time for them. If they had been less engaging with people, their lack of talent might have been more obvious. Instead, they got a reputation for being professional and easygoing; once they appeared on a show, they were always asked back. Both Boyzone and Westlife earned the devotion of fans and the respect of the media by simply being easy to work with.

Well, that's how it started out at least. In the latter years, Boyzone turned moaning and complaining into an Olympic sport.

I like my acts to be pleasant people, who are ambitious and hard-working rather than just super-talented. Aspiring pop stars should remember that those in the industry know that performers are like buses: there's always another one coming along behind.

Look at hugely successful crooner Daniel O'Donnell. He knows that I hate his music, but I have to admire his professionalism. He has a huge and devoted fan base because he's accessible to his fans, he's nice to them and he works hard. That's the secret to his success.

Nice guy Ronan Keating meets Batman's Robin. Or is it nice guy Gary Barlow?

The trick is to keep performers level-headed once fame and fortune arrive. I know it's a cliché, but my music industry motto is: 'Always be nice to everyone on the way up, because you'll meet them all again on the way down.'

It's different in America where the emphasis is on talent rather than decency. I've heard nightmare stories about the likes of Christina Aguilera, Mariah Carey and Beyoncé. That said, Mariah recorded the single 'Against All Odds' with Westlife and they won't hear a bad word about her. They found her perfectly charming and always 'fabulous'.

They can't stand Christina Aguilera. She is extremely talented, ambitious and very professional. Yet I've met few people in the industry who have a good word to say about her. Westlife have no time for her since she tried to have Mark Feehily thrown out of his seat at a club just because she wanted to sit there.

Diana Ross was also very much the diva when she recorded 'When You Tell Me That You Love Me' with Westlife. The guys told me she was very aloof on the set. But they had to admit she's a real professional who delivered on the day. In my eyes Miss Ross is entitled to be a diva because she is a true legend.

The truth is that most of the stars who are there for the long haul tend to be the ones who don't get caught up in their own self-importance. It's no coincidence that Cliff Richard, Tom Jones and Tony Bennett are all hard-working, courteous and totally grounded artists, and still at the top of their game even though they're pensioners and beyond. They know the game and they play it well.

NICENESS

★ 148

Ownership

OWN YOUR MASTERS, MASTER YOUR DESTINY

I'm often asked how U2 got to own all of its recordings and publishing. In the end we paid for it with lower royalties on some of our bestselling work. This autonomy stuff is expensive.

Bono

ROCK ARTISTS U2 are one of the few bands that own their own master tapes ('masters') – the high-quality sound recordings from which millions of records can be pressed – as well as their publishing.

Record contracts usually stipulate that the record companies own the sound recordings or masters. This is the case even though the artist pays for all the recording costs. It gives the record company the right to release and exploit these tapes and to earn broadcast royalties, which they share with the performers.

Because U2 own their masters, they now receive all the broadcast royalties. Or they would if they hadn't leased the masters back to Universal Records. However, this means that at the end of the lease period, the band can choose to up sticks and move to another record company, taking their entire back catalogue with them. They are masters of their own music by owning their masters.

Manager Paul McGuinness fought for U2's masters during a period in which Island Records was facing bankruptcy. In 1985, the label owed the band royalties from their album, *The Unforgettable Fire*, and couldn't pay. The band turned a disaster into an opportunity and got their masters as well as a share of the company. However, Bono has admitted that U2 essentially paid for their recordings by accepting lower royalties on some of their greatest-selling hits.

The issue of ownership and masters appears at the record contract stage. In the past, ownership was automatically assigned to the record companies, but these days, if an artist is in a strong negotiating position, they can follow the example of U2. Or at least they can strike a deal in which the masters are only licensed or leased to the record company for a period of ten or twenty years.

PR
Press Pack
Producers
Promoters
Publicity
Publishers

THE BRIDGE OVER TROUBLED WATERS

> *Teamwork is essential. It allows you to blame someone else.*
>
> Anon

Boyzone's Stephen Gately and his life partner, Andy Cowles.

BOYZONE'S STEPHEN GATELY made the headlines on 16 June 1999 with 'I'm Gay and I'm in Love'. That front page story was staged to the last letter by David and Victoria Beckham's former PR woman, Caroline McAteer, who was with the Outside Organization at the time.

'It all started when someone on tour with Boyzone went to the papers trying to sell the story that Stephen was gay and had a boyfriend,' said Caroline. 'I think everyone in the media and the music industry knew about Stephen's sexuality, but it had never been made public. He had never pretended or denied it, but he never discussed it either. He was worried that the revelations would hurt the band, especially as they were about to launch their greatest hits album.

'I just went through the options with Stephen. Firstly, we could confirm the story. Secondly, we could say nothing but risk this guy selling the story. Denying it was not an option because the truth would have come out. We held the paper off for two weeks and talked it through with Stephen, who decided to tell the story himself. Stephen even got to approve the copy before it was published. We also orchestrated it so that he would be on tour with Boyzone in Italy when it broke so that he was away from all the heat of the situation.'

As you can see, the whole thing was carefully controlled by the Outside Organization and the result was a very positive story. In fact, Stephen's fears were unfounded, and he was overwhelmed by the generous response of the band's fans and fellow celebrities such as Elton John.

THE FAST TRACK TO FLACKS

The PR (public relations) person is also known as a publicist. The slang term used in the US is 'flack', but you'll often hear them called much ruder names by journalists in the UK.

When you're an artist of the stature of U2, Madonna or Britney, you clearly don't need a PR person to get you *in* to the media. The job of a public relations person at this level is to keep you *out* of it. Or at least to control it and fend off bad press. The movers and shakers at the top end of music PR are there more for protection than for publicity; they anticipate and avoid problems. They are essentially the wall that has to be scaled by the media before they reach the artist. See P for Publicity and Promoter.

P
PR

THE ABSOLUTELY FABULOUS IN THE MUSIC PR BUSINESS

Some of the best PRs have a reputation for being ruthless, bullying and manipulative. However, they have to be fearsome to face the voracious appetite of the media. They also have to be tough to handle rich, powerful and spoiled stars. Here are some of those I've worked with and admire.

Alan Edwards of the Outside Organization

His clients include David Bowie, Paul McCartney and Naomi Campbell. He has also worked with Westlife, Elton John, Robbie Williams and the Beckhams.

Barbara Charone of MBC PR

This former music journalist has Madonna on her books. Other A-list clients have included Elton John, REM, Elvis Costello and James Blunt, and she's now handling the Boyzone reunion.

Connie Filippello of Connie Filippello Publicity

Clients include George Michael, Mariah Carey and Donatella Versace. Anyone who can handle these divas has to be good.

Gary Farrow of The Corporation

Gary is one of the best in the UK and has been in the business for more than thirty years. He's old school, extremely smart, a safe pair of hands and deserves a medal because he handles the most fabulous diva of them all, Elton John.

Regine Moylett of RMP London

Regine is one of the most widely respected music PRs in the business and has been with U2 since the Old Testament. She's also Irish and is the sister of Johnny Fingers from the Boomtown Rats. Her client list has also included The Corrs, Sinéad O'Connor, Avril Lavigne and Dido.

Max Clifford of Max Clifford Associates

His clients include Brian McFadden and his majesty Simon Cowell. He's not strictly a music PR, but he's a cool head in a crisis.

Sam Wright of See Saw PR

Former head of promotion at Polydor, Sam is one of the best TV pluggers out there. She was instrumental in Boyzone's success in the UK.

Lindsay Holmes of LHP in Dublin

Lindsay is *the* music PR in Dublin. She works with music artists such as Ronan Keating, Dolores O'Riordan, The Cranberries and U2.

It's an asset if your press photo looks as good as this one of Shakira!

> *We weren't too ambitious when we started out. We just wanted to be the biggest thing that ever walked the planet.*
>
> Steven Tyler of Aerosmith

I GOT TO know Australian singer-songwriter Delta Goodrem through Brian McFadden. She's not only talented, but a really lovely girl to be around. She's also a smart one. When she started out she saw successful music manager Glenn Wheatley as her route to fame.

Unfortunately, Wheatley is deluged with demos every day. So Delta and her mum, Lea, came up with a clever idea. They learned that Wheatley was also a director and part-owner of the Sydney Swans football club. So when this football fanatic spotted a package on his desk wrapped up in a Swan's scarf, he was intrigued enough to play her demo. He later launched Delta as one of the most successful young artists in Australia.

Sometimes it only takes a little creative thinking to make you stand out from the crowd.

Delta's promotional gimmick worked, but she also had the music and the voice to back it up. He would never have signed her if she wasn't a unique talent, but he might never have noticed her in the first place if her demo lay in an anonymous pile in his office.

Your demo (see D for Demos) is part of the press pack that you need to introduce yourself to the world. This is your calling card.

Record companies, publishers, agents and the media are going to see your press pack before they see you. It can also secure gigs, managers, agents – all the professionals in the business. So it'd better be good.

FAST TRACK TO A PRESS PACK

The Photo

The world's a shallow place, so your photo is really important. This is your shop window. If people don't like what they see, they won't come in and look around. Or rather, they're less likely to listen to your demo. I get around 100 demos a week through my office and the record companies; the first thing I look at is the photo. A promotional photo doesn't have to cost a million dollars – it just has to look as though it did. Put some effort, thought and grooming into your photo. And make sure your contact details are on the back.

The Cover Letter

Your press pack should contain a personally addressed cover letter (see below). It is usually written by a manager, but an artist or band frontman can also write it. It's a brief introduction to explain why you are writing to this person, and should contain your contact details.

A. N. Other
Number One Records
Easy Street
London

1 October 2007

Dear A. N. Other,

As the manager of an exciting new boyband called Boyzone, I've enclosed a complete press pack and demo that I hope will interest you.

This pop band has a growing fan base around Ireland, with an exciting live show performed on the nightclub circuit. They've recorded a demo of the Detroit Spinners' hit 'Working My Way Back To You', which I hope you can find time to listen to.

I'll call next week to ensure you've received this pack, and perhaps you would kindly give me some feedback. Please don't hesitate to call if you require further information.

Kind regards,

Louis Walsh
Boyzone manager

The Biography

The biography is your music CV. A single page outline is fine. Include a unique selling point or story if you have one, and briefly detail who you are, what you have done, your music or singing education, and live performance experience, if any. Include your contact details and website or MySpace page.

The Reviews

Include any reviews or press clippings. If you've had verbal feedback from a credible music source, include a few accurate quotes.

The Demo

If the music isn't right, the best press pack in the world won't work. See D for Demos.

FAST TRACK TO FOLLOW-UP

Look who's behind you! Simon Cowell couldn't ignore me forever.

If you've done your research and targeted the right people with a really great press pack, who knows? Maybe they'll contact you. Back in the real world, however, it can take months of calling and leaving messages before you speak to the person you want.

Log all these calls in your big diary book (See P for Publicity) and note who you've talked to and details of the conversation. Persist in making these follow-up calls and keep widening the circle of your campaign. Savage Garden sent out nearly 200 press packs before just two replied. Keep mining, and if you are a really talented act, you'll strike gold.

FAST TRACK TIP

A personal introduction to someone in the music business is worth a thousand phone calls, press packs and press releases.

Simon Cowell refused to take my calls when I was starting out with Boyzone. My press pack clearly didn't do its job! I met him years later at a TV show and he said he didn't speak to me because I was some guy from Ireland he had never heard of. He still ended up signing my next act, Westlife.

You may have a great demo and press pack – the problem is that no one might look at it. Nothing beats personal contact. If you can get an introduction to a person in the music industry, or get your press pack passed on to a record company through a friend or relative, it's worth so much more than an anonymous press pack landing on a desk.

FAST TRACK TO PRESS RELEASES

Your press packs have gone out and you've made the follow-up calls. Now you have to keep in touch with details of gigs or other developments.

A press release should be concise, to the point and easily understood. You can write it by asking yourself: who, what, where and when? **Who** are you? **What** are you doing or **what** is newsworthy? **Where** is it happening and **when?** Then add your contact details and that's a press release.

You should always include your photo with every release – enclose a press photo if you're sending a hard copy, or attach an image if you're sending out emails.

Here is a mock-up of the press release that we sent out for Westlife's first concert in 1998. I met them on 28 February of that year, and with a week's notice they performed with the Backstreet Boys on 17 March.

WESTLIFE

Westlife Support the Backstreet Boys!

New Irish pop group, Westlife, are pleased to announce that they are to support American artists, the Backstreet Boys, at their Dublin concert this weekend.

The recently formed boyband is thrilled with the opportunity to open the show for this international chart-topping act.

'We can't believe that they've asked us to be their support act,' said singer Shane Filan. 'We were going to the concert anyway because we're big fans. It's like a dream that we'll be part of the show!'

Where: RDS, Ballsbridge
When: Tuesday 17 March

For details contact: Louis Walsh (01) XXX XXXX.

FAST TRACK TIP

For details of how to write a press release that will create a buzz in the media, see J for Journalists and Media.

PRODUCERS
THE STUDIO WIZARDS

Infamous producer Phil Spector had a fondness for guns.

PRODUCER PHIL SPECTOR certainly knew how to motivate his artists. He held a loaded pistol to Leonard Cohen's head during the sessions for *Death of a Ladies' Man*. He fired a weapon while in the studio with John Lennon, and he held bass guitarist Dee Dee Ramone of The Ramones at gunpoint until he played to his satisfaction. Johnny Ramone referred to Spector as 'a little man with lifts in his shoes, the wig on top of his head and four guns'.

To give Spector his due, he also wrote and produced the song with the most US radio airplay in the twentieth century: 'You've Lost That Lovin' Feelin' ' by the Righteous Brothers.

Still, who was surprised when it all ended badly. Spector wound up in court in 2007 for the shooting of nightclub hostess and B-movie actress, Lana Clarkson, at his California mansion. Personally, I prefer to work with more stable producers, although sometimes there's a trade-off between genius and madness. Lots of top artists clearly believed that working with Spector and embracing his 'wall of sound' production technique was worth the risk.

Trying to find a producer for Boyzone's first single was an uphill battle. I wasn't known in the pop industry in the UK and the band was an unsigned act. No one would take my calls, until finally I was directed to a producer called Ian Levine, who had made a few great disco singles.

He told us he wanted £10,000, to be paid in advance. That wasn't an outrageous sum at the time, but it was still unfortunate because we didn't have £10. Luckily, a friend of mine, John Reynolds, had the money and agreed to become a partner in Boyzone's management in exchange. So we all went off to London to record the single. The lads had never been to London before. They had never been in a recording studio before . . . and the truth is, most of them were never in a recording studio again!

My heart sank when Levine told me they couldn't sing. He insisted that 'the little blond one' – Ronan Keating – didn't have a note in his head. So we recorded the Detroit Spinners' single, 'Working My Way Back To You', with Mikey Graham and Stephen Gately on lead vocals. It was Mikey's first and last time on lead vocals. Ronan was determined to prove Levine wrong, so we recorded his party piece 'Father and Son' for the B-side for £600. The single was only released in Ireland and went to Number 3.

WHAT DOES A PRODUCER DO?

The producer is the studio wizard who works on the songs, both creatively and technically, to produce a professional recording. A good producer can turn an average sound into a massive hit. Most producers are freelance and work for several record labels and artists; the really successful ones have great contacts in the music business. Of course, these days many producers are now effectively the songwriters as well as producers; most dance acts are self-produced, often using a session singer for lead vocals.

HOW MUCH DO YOU PAY A PRODUCER?

If a successful producer works with a signed artist, he will often get an advance and a percentage of the artist's record royalty. Well-established producers can command royalties of 5–6 per cent of the recommended retail price of the record. An advance will often be paid by the record company, but it still comes out of the artist's royalty payments.

An unsigned act may find a producer who will work for a reduced fee or no fee if he is convinced of their potential. The producer may request a share of future royalties or a contract stating that the act will repay them if they get signed by a record company.

FAST TRACK TO FINDING A PRODUCER

Check CD covers or music notes for details of your favourite artists' producers. The professional body for UK music producers is The Music Producers' Guild. See www. mpg.org.uk; phone (020) 3110 0060. Biographies, discographies and contact numbers for hundreds of US and UK producers are available at www.recordproduction.com. And most music producers are listed in the major music directories (See D for Directories).

The Sugababes are put through their paces in the recording studio.

THE GREAT PRODUCERS

The following are some of the great pop producers I've worked with, admire from a distance or hope to work with some day in the future.

Mutt Lange

The greatest rock 'n' roll producer ever. He's worked with the Boomtown Rats, AC/DC, Foreigner, Def Leppard and The Corrs, and is married to Shania Twain. As Bryan Adams says: 'Mutt Lange could work with my mom and have a hit.'

Steve Mac

Steve is the genius behind some of the best ballads around, including Westlife's biggest hits 'Swear It Again' and 'Flying Without Wings'. He also produced Leona Lewis's 'A Moment Like This', and has worked with artists such as Emma Bunton, Charlotte Church, Atomic Kitten and Kelly Clarkson. He's one of the most successful UK producers and works from his London studios, Rokstone.

Max Martin

One of the best of the many great producers in Sweden, Max is famous for his clever pop choruses and great records that appeal to radio. He has written and produced for Britney Spears, The Backstreet Boys, *NSYNC and Kelly Clarkson.

Rami, Arnthor and Savan

More brilliant Swedish producers and composers, who are currently working as a team with Shayne Ward. Rami Yacoub, Arnthor Birgisson and Savan Kotecha have worked with artists such as Enrique Iglesias, Britney Spears, Backstreet Boys, Westlife, J Lo and Janet Jackson.

To be a great producer, music has to be a big part of your soul.
Brian Wilson, formerly of The Beach Boys

Per Magnusson and David Kreuger

Yes, even more great Swedish producers. They've worked as a team with Boyzone, Westlife and Il Divo.

Rick Rubin

This guru of pop and rock is the antithesis of Phil Spector. He's famous for his stripped-back sound and is more likely to be found in a yoga session with his artists than holding a gun to their heads. He's worked with everyone from the Beastie Boys, Jay Z and the Red Hot Chili Peppers to Neil Diamond, and is responsible for reinventing the legend of Johnny Cash and masterminding his huge hit 'Hurt' with Nine Inch Nails. He's also rumoured to be working on U2's next album.

Brian Higgins

Brian is another successful British producer with his company Xenomania. He's the man behind the sound of both Girls Aloud and the Sugababes. He also wrote songs for Dannii Minogue and gave Cher her monster hit, 'Believe'.

Baby Face

Kenneth 'Baby Face' Edmonds is a huge American R&B and pop success story. He has had 119 Top 10 hits as a writer and producer in the US, sixteen of them Number 1 hits. He has received ten Grammy awards and worked with artists such as Toni Braxton, TLC, Boyz II Men, Madonna, Michael Jackson, Janet Jackson, Whitney Houston, Celine Dion and Eric Clapton.

Jam & Lewis

James 'Jimmy Jam' Harris and Terry Lewis are the team behind Janet Jackson's success: they produced all her big hits, 'What Have You Done For Me Lately', 'Nasty', 'Whoops Now' and 'Scream'. They have also worked with Jessica Simpson, Mariah Carey, Mary J. Blige and Bryan Adams.

David Foster

This Canadian is a legend in the American music industry. He's won fourteen Grammy awards and been nominated for more than forty, and has worked with all the greats, from Barbra Streisand and Michael Jackson, to Destiny's Child and Madonna. On this side of the Atlantic, The Corrs were one of the few acts lucky enough to work with him.

PROMOTERS
THE MUSIC GAMBLERS

PROMOTERS PUT UP with a lot. Aerosmith frontman, Steven Tyler, and his bandmates trashed the backstage area during their first Japanese tour. And why exactly did these grown men throw a massive tantrum? The Japanese promoter had been remiss with their buffet table. 'I explicitly said, "No turkey roll!" ' said Tyler.

Promoters assume the financial risk when putting on a show – they are the gamblers in the music business, which makes them a lot like the record companies. They place their faith in an act, commit their money and stage a show. However, if they've overestimated the popularity of an artist, they can lose their shirt.

Former Mean Fiddler promoter, Vince Power, did very well on the London music scene, so decided to go home to Ireland to show people just how successful he was. He decided to stage a star-studded festival in Tramore, a small seaside town in Ireland, featuring legends such as Bob Dylan and Ray Charles.

Promoters can even lose their shirts on music legends like Bob Dylan.

The festival cost a fortune to produce, and in the end not enough people turned up to meet the costs. He estimates he lost £2 million – and that was back in 1993 when £2 million meant something. However, don't worry, Vince hasn't exactly been living under a bridge ever since. He sold his Mean Fiddler company for £40 million in 2006, and now you'll find him in the directory under the Vince Power Music Group (VPMG).

WHAT DOES A PROMOTER DO?

In the past, it was simple. Promoters hired the performers, paid a deposit for the venue, printed the posters, organized the advertising and hired the staff needed to run the show. They then made a handsome profit by selling tickets. These days, it's a bit different, because many promoters own live music venues.

THE RISE OF THE SUPERPROMOTER

Across the US, many local promoters have been bought out by billion dollar companies like Clear Channel. This company has huge influence and control over the live music market in America, because they also own many of the venues, radio stations and advertising companies.

Arthur Fogel of Clear Channel Music Group and Michael Cohl of CPI are the top international tour agents, producers and promoters in the world. Cohl started the whole 'superpromoter' concept by paying the Rolling Stones a $60 million advance for their 'Steel Wheels' world tour in 1989. In return he got the concerts, sponsorship, merchandise, radio, TV and film rights.

Arthur Fogel handles world tours for artists such as U2, Madonna, Sting, David Bowie and Neil Young. He works for a company that can bankroll the huge production costs of a megatour and issue artist guarantees of more than $100–200 million. This means the big artists and their managers only have to deal with one person, rather than negotiating with dozens of individual promoters whose only concerns are their local markets. Fogel's attention to detail is legendary: he ensures that Bowie gets his favourite brand of coffee backstage every night, and he attended every show all over the world on U2's 'Vertigo' tour.

Promoters vie with each other for acts like Madonna.

HOW DOES A PROMOTER STAGE A SHOW?

If a major artist such as Christina Aguilera is planning a tour, every major promoter will contact her agent and will compete with each other by offering guaranteed fees. The agent will look at all the offers and negotiate the best deal for her.

Agents will know that some artists, such as Bono, never perform more than two shows in succession to ensure their voice is never strained on tour. They will then chart concert dates into a geographically logical order and work out a European tour, American tour, Asian tour, etc.

In the case of a new artist, promoters are not going to be knocking down the door, so the artist's agent must get to work and call them. He or she tries to pitch the performer or band and secure a series of dates. If the artist is successful and sells tickets, the agent will have an easier job the next time they set out to get gigs for their client.

TOP PROMOTERS

I've only ever worked with the best. John Giddings of Solo is an agent, but as part of Clear Channel is really our promoter in the UK too. In Ireland I work with the two big promoters: Peter Aiken of Aiken Promotions and Denis Desmond of MCD. Promoter John Reynolds co-managed Boyzone with me back in the good old days. John, who runs the successful Electric Picnic festival, is a great friend as well as a great promoter. Another promoter with great tales of the industry is Pat Egan; he's been around as long as I have.

BAD PUBLICITY? WHAT BAD PUBLICITY?

▶ Who'd have guessed a Disney Mouseketeer could turn into sexy pop superstar, Christina Aguilera?

> *Early to bed, early to rise, work like hell and advertise.*
>
> Ted Turner

THERE'S A WELL-KNOWN TV clip featuring Boyzone's first appearance on *The Late Late Show*, which is the biggest TV programme in Ireland. The original Boyzone appeared on the show just a day or two after they were formed. They had no songs, but the presenter, Gay Byrne, insisted that they perform on the live show. So the guys decided to dance. They had no experience in putting together a slick choreography routine, and ended up with a gyrating, lunging and crotch-grabbing disaster, performed to the backing tape of the song 'Burn Baby Burn'. It was absolutely excruciating, and still appears on comedy shows around the world today.

And the reason you can see it on shows such as *It Shouldn't Happen to a Pop Star* is because I always sign the release forms for it to appear on TV. Yes, they were dreadful, but they were on national TV. People might have been laughing at them, but at least they were being talked about. I think after that bit of public humiliation, it made the guys more determined to prove themselves.

I enjoy seeing that clip. I think it shows what hard work, ambition and grooming can achieve. Look at early videos of Christina Aguilera, Britney Spears and Justin Timberlake too, and you'd never guess you were looking at future superstars. I firmly believe that there's no such thing as bad publicity. With the noted exception of Gary Glitter-type revelations, **the only really bad publicity for an artist is no publicity.**

MEDIA PROMOTION AND PLUGGERS

There's a sign hanging in the office of U2 manager, Paul McGuinness. It reads: 'Something terrible happens if you don't promote: Nothing.'

U2 have had success beyond most artists' dreams, but with every release they still get out there and promote.

TV advertising, radio play and exposure in the national press is what every artist needs to sell records and tickets. Acts signed to a record company work with people called 'pluggers' to get their music on radio or reviewed in the media. A plugger's job is to liaise with their contacts in the media and get publicity for their artists.

DIY PROMOTION

Unsigned acts won't have the help of a record company, but they can still get publicity. The key to successful promotion is research and creativity. There's no point sending your demo to Radio 1's Chris Moyles, for example, unless you're Robbie Williams.

However, there are radio producers and DJs who welcome demos from new artists. Similarly, there are youth TV shows that may be interested in an exciting new act. You simply contact the producer of the show with your press pack and a video. Local and regional newspapers may also be interested.

Music and style magazines always want to find the next big thing and will generate buzz about talented artists. A write-up in an influential music magazine such as *Hit Box*, which championed Corinne Bailey Rae, is a huge boon to any unsigned artist. Also check out style magazines like *i-D* and *Dazed & Confused*.

Just remember that promotion involves a lot of hard work; it's the part of the business that even successful artists hate. For unsigned acts, self-promotion involves lots of knock-backs, unanswered phone messages, fob offs, sheer frustration and research, research, research. Stop thinking about it and just do it.

It's so good we'll say it twice: **'Something terrible happens if you don't promote: Nothing.'**

▶ Corinne Bailey Rae's early career got a boost when she was championed by music magazine, Hit Box.

FAST TRACK TIP TO SUCCESSFUL DIY PROMOTION

Get yourself a contacts book and a big diary. As soon as you put down the phone, leave a message or leave a meeting, record the details of the call or meeting and who you spoke to in your diary. Note their number carefully in your contacts book. When you send out press packs or demos, make a note of who they are sent to. Then keep notes of the follow-up calls. It's easy to get confused when you're constantly talking to different people in different companies. The only way to stay on top of it is to keep notes of everything in your big book. Then, when you call people, you can say, 'I talked to you last Friday week and you suggested that I call you back around this time', as if you remember every detail of the call. See also I for Internet, J for Journalists and Media, P for Press Pack and L for Live Performing for more ideas on DIY promotion.

PROFESSIONAL PROMOTIONS

Promotion through advertising, professional pluggers and PR people is expensive. There's no point in even thinking of taking on professional help unless (a) you have the money and (b) you are putting out your own record and are truly convinced it could be a huge hit. There are independent pluggers and music PR people who work for smaller labels and unsigned artists for a fee. Finding the right PR company takes a lot of careful research, but finding the funds is probably a bigger problem. It costs many thousands of pounds to pay for the services of a professional PR company.

PR PACKAGES

Black Dog Promotions is an international music promotion company that offers PR packages to get artists featured and listed on major indie music sites and e-zines. They'll also submit press releases to local, regional and national music-industry publications. They sell CDs through their online store and send out bi-monthly newsletters and press releases. There is a three-month promotional package for $599 (£300) or six months for $999 (£500). They have a Myspace marketing plan to help you gain 5,000 to 10,000 Myspace friends costing $599 (£300).

STREET TEAMS

Street teams are groups of fans who work together to promote a band at grass-roots level on the streets by handing out fliers, selling tickets for shows, or calling radio shows and requesting airplay for their favourite band's new single. There are also eTeams, which are groups of fans who spread the word about a band online. They talk-up the artist on chat and message sites, through email, etc. Many record companies use street teams to promote their acts. Roadrunner Records in the UK actively recruit

FAST TRACK TIP TO PROFESSIONAL HELP

Check out the online Showcase International Music Book for lists of PRs and pluggers at www.showcase-music.com. You may also find it in your local library or you can buy it for £70. Phone (020) 8973 3400.

them for their artists. Team members are usually rewarded with exclusive news, tickets or merchandise of their band. You can set up your own street team as soon as you have a willing fan base. However, you can also pay professional street-team management companies who will mobilize teams in your name. Companies like Fancorps in the US offer street-team packages from $15 (£7.50) to $300 (£150) a month. In the UK there are companies like **trafficonline.net** and **xtaster.co.uk** doing the same thing.

FAST TRACK WARNING

Irish singer, Carly Hennessy, was just fifteen or sixteen when she landed a huge record deal with MCA in America. She was dubbed the Irish answer to Britney Spears, and MCA's confidence in her was rewarded when she produced a fantastic début rock-pop album called *Ultimate High*. Her future as an international star appeared assured.

The album stiffed. Why? It was released the day before the 11 September terrorist attacks, and no one was interested during the turmoil that followed.

The record company was also undergoing a major shake-up at the time and Carly fell between the cracks. The following January, she appeared on the front page of the *Wall Street Journal* described as a multi-million-dollar music flop. Sometimes you can do everything right, but forces way beyond your control can make it all go awry.

DON'T FORGET THE G.A.Y. ROUTE

The Spice Girls did their very first PA in G.A.Y. nightclub in London, which has provided a springboard to fame for many emerging acts. Kylie performed there back in 1993, and her sister Dannii is now a regular at the club. Pussycat Dolls were launched in the UK in G.A.Y. and Girls Aloud also had their first gig there. 'We're always looking for the next big act and we support them from the very beginning,' says club boss Jeremy Joseph. 'It's very important for pop acts, because in many cases they have never performed before an adult audience before. It's also a way for the acts to get to that audience and develop a gay fan base. Acts who appear here usually make headlines too, because we encourage them to do things they wouldn't do before their traditional audience. McFly stripped off naked on stage and they couldn't buy the kind of coverage they got! Amy Winehouse is coming here tonight – who knows what will end up in the papers on Monday?' Any emerging act should grab the chance to perform at G.A.Y., although Jeremy Joseph is notoriously choosy about who gets on stage. Only those acts with huge advance buzz about them will get a spot.

PUBLISHERS
THE SONG MANAGERS

BACK IN 1980, U2 still weren't signed to a record label and needed to finance a tour. As a result, they almost signed over their songs to a music publisher for a paltry $3,000 advance. However, the publisher discovered that they badly needed the money and halved the advance.

He could have had control of U2's songs for years if he had stuck to his original offer. But he lost out on the publishing deal of a lifetime because U2 told him where he could stick his $1,500.

WHAT IS A MUSIC PUBLISHER?

A publisher is a manager of songs. You will only require a publisher if you write your own music. There is serious money to be made in the business if you are an accomplished songwriter. Diane Warren in the US is so successful she runs her own publishing outfit, Realsongs, and tells me she's worth 250 million – I think that's dollars, but who cares? For more about Diane see S for Songwriting.

A music publisher is essentially a manager of songs, whose job it is to maximize the earning power of a song, to collect the earnings and pay the songwriter. You sign over copyright to your songs when you sign with a publisher, and he or she then goes to work selling your music to third parties. A good publisher will try to sell your music to their influential contacts in TV, radio and movies, as well as other artists. He or she will then track down all the income your songs are generating from different sources and different regions of the world. They are also likely to pay you an advance – just like a record company – to keep you going until your songwriting career becomes successful. However, publishing deals are not usually as lucrative as recording deals.

Many record companies are affiliated with, or have their own, publishing companies. Examples include Warners/Chappell Publishing, EMI Music Publishing and Universal Music Publishing.

HOW DOES A PUBLISHER COLLECT SONGWRITERS' MONEY?

Publishers are members of collection societies, such as MCPS (Mechanical Copyright Protection Society) in the UK and Ireland, PRS (Performing Right Society) in the UK, or IMRO (Irish Music Rights Organization) in Ireland. The former collects money owed to songwriters from record companies every time a CD is sold. The latter collect money owed to songwriters when their songs are performed on stage or played on TV and radio. Publishers use these collection societies to collect their clients' money.

See C for Collection Societies and Copyright and R for Royalties.

DO YOU NEED A PUBLISHER?

A songwriter can join the aforementioned collection societies without a publisher. However, a good publisher is much more than just a collection agent. He or she should actively market your songs for adverts, TV, films and other chart-topping artists.

They will also try to team you with other songwriters and try to improve your skills. Some of the bigger publishing houses even have their own studios to help you prepare top-quality demos and land a record deal. If you get a record deal first, it will usually follow that you will get a publishing deal.

Major publishers will also have representatives or sub-publishers in territories around the world, ensuring that your songs and royalties are properly tracked.

HOW MUCH DO YOU PAY A PUBLISHER?

Never pay a publisher upfront. The publisher takes a share of all the income received – mechanical and performance royalties – from your songwriting (see R for Royalties). This share can be as high as 50 per cent for a new songwriter or as little as 5 per cent or less for a superstar songwriter. However, deductions are normally in the region of 20–40 per cent.

FAST TRACK TO FINDING A PUBLISHER

Look through your CD collection and find details of the companies that publish music you like or that is similar to your material.

Alternatively, you can also search the free online directory of the Music Publishers' Association in the UK. You can search by genre of music, and can also find out which publishers will accept unsolicited material. See www.mpaonline.org.uk.

The Music Publishers' Association of Ireland (MPAI) can be contacted at Copyright House, Pembroke Row, Lower Baggot Street, Dublin 2; phone (01) 676 6940.

Identify the A&R scout or person within the publishing company that you need to deal with and send them a simple demo of no more than three songs, with lyrics printed separately. See C for Copyright for details of how to protect your music before you send it out into the world. British Music Rights represents the copyright interests of publishers, composers and songwriters. See www.bmr.org.

FAST TRACK WARNING

Some publishers refuse to accept unsolicited demos. EMI Publishing explain that they are protecting themselves from writers claiming that the songs they submitted were 'stolen' and given to other writers to work on.

Q

Qualifications

STAGE SCHOOL OR SCHOOL OF HARD KNOCKS?

JOE AND MARIE Lewis spent tens of thousands of pounds on drama school and stage school fees for their daughter, Leona. *X Factor* winner Leona Lewis attended the Sylvia Young Theatre School in London, at a cost of up to £8,400 in annual fees. There she instantly joined a hall of fame that includes Emma Bunton

> *I only got seventh-grade education, but I have a doctorate in funk and I like to put that to good use.*
> James Brown

of the Spice Girls, and All Saints' chart-toppers Melanie Blatt and Nicole and Natalie Appleton. Leona also attended the expensive Italia Conti Academy of Theatre Arts; my own good pal Sharon Osbourne is one of their ex-pupils. Leona's parents finally got a break when she was fourteen and won a place at the only free performing arts school in the UK: the famous BRIT School in Croydon in London, where Leona shared a star-studded roll call with Amy Winehouse and Katie Melua.

And wasn't all the money her parents forked out for her education well spent when she went on to win *X Factor* 2006? Absolutely.

Shayne Ward also won *X Factor* in 2005, but he never had so much as a single singing, drama or dance lesson. Instead, he learned his trade by performing for four and a half years with a small pop trio called Destiny. He also has natural ability, a great personality and good looks.

Ronan Keating didn't go to stage school either, but was part of a teenage pop band called Namaste. He also loves music and has a great work ethic, as well as Irish charm!

Both Shayne and Ronan are examples of how you can succeed, even if you don't have the same opportunities as others. Their achievements are proof that hard work, drive and ambition are the essential ingredients for success.

TO LEARN OR NOT TO LEARN

An expensive stage school or performing arts education (or even a free one if you manage to attend the BRIT School) is no guarantee of pop fame and fortune. However, no education or training is ever wasted. **You should never pass up the opportunity to learn to play a musical instrument or read music, take dance lessons or attend drama classes.** Every dimension you add to your talent can open up more exciting opportunities for an artist.

Simon Cowell works his legendary charm on Leona Lewis.

Classes also allow you to make contact with like-minded people, and casting agents regularly trawl stage schools to recruit young trainees for movies, stage shows, TV soaps and adverts.

The experience you gain can certainly give you an edge when you are pursuing a career in the music or entertainment industry.

THE BRIT SCHOOL

The BRIT School is the only state-funded, free performing arts school in the UK. Entry into the school is at fourteen, or at sixteen after completion of GCSEs. It accepts students from most of Greater London, as well as parts of Kent and Surrey, but it only takes a small percentage of students from other parts of the country.

The BRIT School is located at **60 The Crescent, Croydon, CRO 2HN**. See **www.brit. croydon.sch.uk**; phone **(020) 8665 5242**.

PART-TIME TRAINING FOR STARDOM

Budding stars don't need to attend expensive full-time performing arts schools. They can always brush up on their skills at local stage, drama or music schools that hold classes after school, at weekends and during the holidays.

Brian McFadden, Boyzone's Mikey Graham and Samantha Mumba all learned the basics of singing and dancing at the famous Billie Barry Stage School in Dublin. There's little doubt that their years of performing and training gave them an extra edge at auditions.

To find a music teacher, try the extensive directories available at www.musicteachers.co.uk, www.musiclessonsonline.co.uk, and the Incorporated Society of Musicians at www.ism.org. They allow you to search for lessons in the instrument of your choice, including vocals, in your local area. In Ireland, music teachers, schools and classes can be found at www.learnmusic.info.

You should also check out 'music schools' on www.yell.com in the UK or www.goldenpages.ie in Ireland.

FAST TRACK TO MUSIC QUALIFICATIONS

Access to Music

Access to Music has a range of courses for children and adults, from full-time higher education courses, to part-time courses at weekends and evenings. Most courses are funded by the Learning and Skills Council, which means you can access them free of charge, or at a subsidized rate. All courses are custom-designed by musicians for musicians. See **www.accesstomusic.co.uk**.

Music Education Directory

The Music Education Directory is a useful internet resource for anyone considering further education in music in the UK or Ireland. It contains details and contacts of more than 500 recognized courses, from the technical to the creative – everything from a ten-week course in audio engineering in Alchemea in London, to the famous Rock School in Ballyfermot College in Dublin. Many of the best music and music industry courses in the UK and Ireland are available at a glance at **www.bpi-med.co.uk**.

Hot Courses

Also try **www.hotcourses.com**, which features useful reviews from former students for many courses in the UK.

Grants are available for those over the age of sixteen in some of the leading private dance, drama and performing arts schools around the UK. See the 'Money to Learn' link on the government site www.direct.gov.uk/educationandlearning. See also The Educational Grants Directory 2006/07 by Alan French and Tom Traynor, which details funding for children and students up to degree level. Try your local library, or order it from the Directory of Social Change at www.dsc.org.uk for £34.95.

▶ Gareth Gates got early training as a member of the Bradford Cathedral Choir.

Record Companies
Rehearsing
Riders
Royalties

RECORD COMPANIES
MAKING THE BUSINESS GO ROUND

> *What pisses me off is when I've got seven or eight record company fat pig men sitting there telling me what to wear.*
>
> Sinéad O'Connor

WHEN I DECIDED to manage Westlife, I hoped to get them signed to Sony. We held a showcase for Rob Stringer, the CEO of Sony, at the Red Box in Dublin. The band sang their hearts out and all seemed to be terrific. He appeared to really like the guys. He told us everything was great and he'd be in touch.

So we were all pretty chuffed. Then I got a phone call from the driver who'd taken Stringer back to Dublin airport. Rob didn't realize that Dublin is such a small town. The driver had overheard him making a call to Sony's head office in London and telling them that Westlife were 'nothing special' and 'just another boyband'.

I knew then that we wouldn't get a deal with Sony. Still, it was Rob's loss. Westlife went on to sell 40 million albums for BMG. The moral of the story is: never believe record industry hype until you are actually presented with a contract. **No one says 'no' in this business. Instead, they don't say 'yes'.**

So take heart if you get knocked back, because you're in good company. Legends such as the Beatles and U2 were turned down in the past, too. The Decca Recording Company, along with nearly every other record label, rejected the Beatles in 1962. 'We don't like their sound,' explained Decca. 'Groups of guitars are on the way out.' Two years later, the Beatles' singles were at Numbers 1, 2, 3, 4 and 5 in the UK charts.

Rockers U2 even donated two record company rejection letters to the Rock and Roll Hall of Fame in Cleveland, USA. One is a rejection slip sent to Bono by RSO records, or more accurately 'Mr. P. Hewson', in May 1979. The slip informs Bono that the demo tape he sent to the label was 'not suitable for us at present'. Coincidentally, the RSO letter bears the same date as Bono's nineteenth birthday, and was signed by the label's unfortunate A&R man, Alexander Sinclair. The exhibition also contains a brief, standard rejection letter from Arista Records from around the same time.

Remember: rejection happens to the best of us. It toughens you up.

FAST TRACK TO MAJORS AND INDIES

You'll invariably hear record companies referred to as 'majors' or 'indies'. The big four 'majors' are Warner Music Group, EMI, Sony BMG and Universal Music Group. Between them they control an estimated 70 per cent of the world music market and about 80 per cent of the US market.

However, within these four are hundreds of other labels known as 'imprints'. For example, Universal Music Group owns well-known labels such as Island Records, Def Jam, Mercury, Polydor, Geffen and Interscope.

If you belong to any record label that is not owned by these four, you are signed to an 'indie' or independent record company.

MAJORS OR INDIES?

Ex-Sony records boss, Tommy Mottola, wanted airtime for a little-known Latin artist at the biggest music event of the American calendar – the Grammy Awards – back in 1999. So he threatened to withhold all future appearances of Destiny's Child and J Lo unless a singer called Ricky Martin featured in the broadcast. The rest, is history.

The big record companies have so much clout that they may indeed propel you to dizzy heights in the music world. However, a new artist on a successful label may just as easily be overshadowed by the other stars on its roster, and may be better off signing to a smaller indie label, which will concentrate a lot of its resources and its full attention on its new signing.

HOW DO YOU GET A RECORD DEAL?

Ricky Martin propelled to fame with the muscle of a major.

The best way to get a record deal is to – literally – have your act together. Green Day never went looking for a record deal; the record companies came to them because they had built a big fan base in their local area and were selling their own CDs.

If you're an artist, you have to create advance buzz about yourself. You can do that on the internet, through the media and by performing live. The record company wants to see artists that are already connecting with an audience. You also need a killer demo and a professional manner. If you've achieved all this, the record companies usually come to you.

Remember: it only takes one person in the record company to believe in you to get everyone else in the label on your side.

If you decide to approach a record company, don't do it too early. You may only get one chance, so don't blow it by not being ready. The A&R department is the door into the record company. Smaller labels may use a more informal network of talent scouting, through DJs, producers and owners of music venues. See A for A&R.

RECORD COMPANY FEEDBACK

Your aunt's neighbour's friend happens to know the receptionist in a record company? Great! If someone can place the demo into the A&R's hands on your behalf, you have a much better chance of someone listening to it. Use every bit of pull or influence you possibly can to reach the right people.

An unknown backing singer persuaded an artist with Columbia Records to give her demo to the record company boss in 1989. Head of Columbia, Tommy Mottola, listened to it in his car. That's how the megastar Mariah Carey was born.

If you don't have any contacts, it can be hard work and very frustrating trying to get a response from the record companies. All you ever get are automated answerphones. If you do manage to speak to a human being, the standard response is 'they're in a meeting'. And the reasons they don't call back are because (a) they're too busy or can't be bothered listening to your demo, or (b) they've heard it and are not that excited but don't want to say 'no'.

If it's (a), and you suspect they haven't heard your demo, then persist until they at least listen to it. If it's (b), and they tell you they've listened to it but they're still not waving a contract under your nose, then maybe it's time to move on to another label. People in record companies often don't want to be seen saying 'no'.

Scissor Sisters' huge European success is due to Lucian Grainge of Universal.

FAST TRACK TO FINDING RECORD COMPANIES

You'll find an exhaustive list of UK record companies and contact numbers at www. showcasemusic.com. There's more information, including links to record companies' websites, at www.musicweek.com. You have to register, but access to that part of the directory is free. Details of UK and Irish record companies and their website links are also available on the music industry database www.firstmusiccontact.com.

Alternatively, you'll find full record company listings in the music directories discussed in D for Directories, and often available in your local library.

RECORD COMPANY LEGENDS

This is my list of the best in the record business.

Lucian Grainge of Universal

Universal is the umbrella group for labels such as Polydor, Island and Mercury. They don't get much bigger in the record industry than Lucian; he will go down in UK record history as a legend. He controls 80 per cent of the UK record charts and wants more, more, more! Even as I write he has seven albums in the Top 10, but I bet he won't be happy until all ten are his. He masterminded stardom for acts such as Keane, Scissor Sisters, Amy Winehouse, The Feeling, Jamie Cullum and Boyzone. He's one of the few who doesn't just talk – he does.

Clive Davis of J Records

He's the guy I most look up to. He's a 'songs' man, and the most influential individual in the American music business by a mile. He loves music across every genre – country, R&B, rock, pop. He's made more stars than anyone else – Chicago, Dionne Warwick, Whitney Houston, Bruce Springsteen, Barry Manilow, Alicia Keys, Santana, Sarah McLachlan – the list is endless. He's another legend. He's still going strong, even in his seventies, and the hits keep coming.

Simon Cowell of Sony BMG

The thing about Simon is that he hates any kind of failure. He's so competitive. No one could have made a better success of making and breaking Westlife than he did. He was on top of everything. And he always knows a hit song when I bring it to him.

Colin Barlow of Polydor

He's joint MD with David Joseph, and has always been a terrific person to work with. He signed many of my acts, including Boyzone, Samantha Mumba, Ronan Keating and Girls Aloud. He has enthusiasm, drive and vision, and knows the industry inside out.

▶ Avril Lavigne's multi-platinum sales are a tribute to American music industry legend, L. A. Reid.

David Joseph of Polydor

He's the new kid on the block who is being groomed for stardom. He's passionate and excited about his projects and has a fantastic team around him. He has overseen important signings, such as Scissor Sisters, Snow Patrol, Kaiser Chiefs and James Morrison, and orchestrated the Take That comeback.

Sonny Takhar of Syco Records

Sonny is Simon Cowell's business partner in Syco, which is the biggest little label in the UK. He works with Shayne Ward, Westlife, Il Divo and Leona Lewis. He's young, energetic and ambitious, and can handle every detail, from the photographs to the songs – he's very hands-on.

Ged Doherty of Sony BMG

Like all the best in the business, Ged has worked his way up. He's been a booker, a promoter, and managed acts such as Paul Young and Alison Moyet in the eighties. Then he stormed through the industry ranks to become the head of one of the 'big four': Sony BMG.

Craig Logan of Sony BMG

An ex-member of Bros, he won a £1 million dispute over royalties with Matt and Luke Goss. He went to work with Roger Davies Management, where he managed Pink, then moved to sales in EMI, and is now in charge of the RCA record label, where he signed Sandi Thom and looks after George Michael. He's one of the new breed, who appreciates great songs, has huge ability and is loved by his artists.

L. A. Reid of Island Def Jam Music Group

L. A. Reid is the most powerful black man in the music industry. The former head of Arista Records, now head of Island Def Jam Music Group, he's worked with artists such as Mariah Carey, Whitney Houston, Outkast, Usher and Avril Lavigne. Having started out as an artist, he cares more about music than he does about the music business.

Tommy Mottola, co-owner of Casablanca Records

The larger-than-life former head of Sony was at one stage the most influential man in American music. Michael Jackson called him 'the devil', but Mottola created some of the biggest music divas in the business, including Mariah Carey, Celine Dion, J Lo and Destiny's Child. He also married Mariah Carey, but don't mention the war. Other artists he has worked with include Shakira, Dixie Chicks, Bruce Springsteen and Billy Joel. He resurrected Casablanca – an old eighties record label that once boasted the glam rock act Kiss – in a joint venture with Universal in 2004. One of his first signings was Lindsay Lohan, who has since moved to Motown, and he's currently enjoying big success with Mika.

REHEARSING
PRACTICE MAKES PERFECT

REHEARSING IS MUSIC'S version of studying. If you want to be a major star, prepare to do your swotting; you will need to rehearse, rehearse some more, and then rehearse, rehearse and rehearse again. There are no shortcuts, even if you are a music genius.

U2 have been performing together for thirty years. Yet they still record performances and review them in order to see how they can improve their shows. There's nothing like live performing to sharpen and develop your stage skills. If you get out there too fast, you'll lose your confidence and your audience, and find yourself back at square one.

I can't emphasize how important it is to rehearse, to record your rehearsals, to watch those rehearsals, and to start all over again. **When you're bored to death of rehearsing, set a date for your first show – friends and family only – for six months' time. Then get back to rehearsing.**

Don't rush things. It's going to be a long time before you're ready to take on L for Live Performing or D for Demos.

AT WHAT STAGE CAN I USE THE RECORDING STUDIO?

Don't set foot in a recording studio until you are so well rehearsed that you could perform in your sleep. This is not the place to be tuning up, bickering over songs or trying out new guitar solos. Studio time costs you money, and lots of it. Even if you're lucky enough to have a record company to cover the costs, you will ultimately be paying that bill. Rehearsal studios are a lot cheaper than recording studios, so use them for waffling and for discussing your artistic differences.

WHEN DO I NEED TO USE REHEARSAL STUDIOS?

When the neighbours call in the Environmental Health Department about the noise, it may be time to start thinking about hiring rehearsal studios. A dedicated rehearsal room is the only place in which you're definitely not going to be yelled at to 'turn that racket down!'

> *If you're gonna treat music like a hobby, go f**king work at Starbucks.*
>
> Steven Tyler of Aerosmith

Some communities have local halls and centres that they will rent out for rehearsals. There are also purpose-designed rehearsal rooms for hire. These can range from a bare garage where you are expected to bring all your own gear, to well-equipped rehearsal rooms that are fully soundproofed, with the added luxury of heating and coffee facilities.

Stars like Gwen Stefani rehearse, rehearse and rehearse again.

HOW MUCH DO REHEARSAL ROOMS COST?

Rehearsal rooms usually cost between £8 and £12 an hour, depending on location and facilities. Bush Studios in Shepherd's Bush in London charges £8 per hour. See **www.bushstudios.co.uk**; phone **(020) 8740 1740**. The Complete Sound Rehearsal Studio in Warwickshire charges £9 per hour. See **www.completesoundrehearsalstudio.com**; phone **(01926) 833445**. Vertebrae Studios in Terenure in Dublin charges from €55 to € 60 for four-hour sessions only. See **www.vstudios.ie**; phone **087 774 9859**.

FAST TRACK TIP TO FINDING REHEARSAL ROOMS

Sign up free to access *Music Week*'s directory at www.musicweek.com, which has complete listings of rehearsal studios across the UK. Also check music magazines such as *NME* and *Hot Press*, and papers like *Loot*. See www.yell.com in the UK or www.goldenpages.ie in Ireland for comprehensive listings in your area. See also D for Directories.

THE CHERRY ON THE CAKE

I like to have six Coca-Colas when I get to the building. I don't need a dressing room. You can put a curtain up, I don't care.

Elvis Presley's early backstage demands

SUPERSTAR ARTISTS CAN look forward to being pampered on tour. They travel first class or by private jet; they are chauffeured to one five-star hotel after another; and backstage is all lobster buffets, champagne on ice, ping-pong tables and roses. While emerging artists are lucky to get a clean towel at a concert venue, big stars get to demand personal perks known as a 'rider' in a contract.

A rider lists all the dull production requirements for staging an artist's show, such as how many stage crew or 'humpers' are required to unload the convoy of trucks and pack it up again, as well as details of how many guest tickets are required. It also contains the frivolous personal demands and whims of pampered celebrities. Riders can include everything from demands for the presidential suite of five-star hotels to cans of sardines.

▶ An unusual rider request but if P. Diddy wants to be carried aloft in a golden litter, the promoter will arrange it!

According to newspaper reports, Mick demanded an internet connection or satellite television backstage during the Rolling Stones' 'Bigger Bang' tour. He brought his own TV on tour, but required a little local help from the promoters. 'Please find out what channel is showing cricket,' read the rider. 'That is the channel we need most of all.'

Specific travel arrangements are also included in some riders. Many artists like to demand the window seat in the last row of first class so that they can see everyone, but everyone else has to turn around to see them.

Rockers Van Halen famously included a provision calling for a bowl of M&Ms with all the brown sweets removed. And they wrecked the backstage area when they found the offending colour. Lead singer David Lee Roth later claimed that the sweetie clause was in the contract to ensure the promoter had actually gone to the trouble of reading it. He insisted their production was so heavy that for safety reasons they needed the contract to be followed to the letter.

Of course, many of the demands on riders are made by the tour managers and people around the artist. They are often bigger divas than the artists themselves and are always trying to prove their worth to the artist with ridiculous demands. You can ask for anything you want on tour when you reach superstar status. However, before you start dreaming up some diva demands, you should remember that you end up paying for it all yourself. Many artists don't realize this until it's too late and the money is all gone!

▶ Gifts (even a double bed) will be showered at Christina Aguilera's feet if she requests them as part of her rider.

ROYALTIES
THE ETERNAL FLAME

ROYALTIES ARE ONE of the most important sources of income for music stars, and the real beauty is that they will keep rolling in for decades, long after your pop career is over. Royalties are also the reason why even really successful pop acts like Westlife, Kylie Minogue and Britney Spears can never make the same money as U2, the Rolling Stones and Elton John.

Mick Jagger and Keith Richards get plenty of Satisfaction where royalties are concerned.

Singer-songwriters make far more in royalties, which are generated every time their music is recorded, broadcast or performed in public. **Many were gobsmacked when it was revealed that the Rolling Stones earned £242 million in royalties alone over the past twenty years.** The figure was divulged for legal reasons, but it gives you some idea of the money that can be earned by superstar acts.

Mick Jagger and Keith Richards, the songwriters in the group, would have made most of that money, and they need never worry about this income running out. Songwriters' royalties roll in for the duration of their lives, and seventy years afterwards. Their heirs can expect to collect royalty cheques probably until the end of this century.

However, their fellow Stones – Charlie Watts and Ronnie Wood – only perform on the recordings. Performers receive different royalties to songwriters, and they only own copyright of their performances for fifty years. The current law allows anyone to use music recordings after fifty years without paying a penny in royalties.

Charlie Watts was with the band in the sixties, so some of his early recordings with the Stones will fall out of copyright in a few years' time. Jagger and Richards will also

> *It isn't necessary to be rich and famous to be happy.*
> *It's only necessary to be rich.*
>
> Alan Alda

lose these performers' royalties, but they will still have their songwriting royalties.

Many artists, including U2 star Bono, have joined forces in a campaign to keep recording royalties rolling in long after the fifty-year deadline. They want to extend copyright protection for sound recordings to the ninety-five years adopted in America in 1998. Most countries outside Europe offer at least seventy years' protection.

FAST TRACK TO ROYALTIES

There are four sources of royalties. If you are a singer you receive two types of royalty; if you are a songwriter you receive the other two forms. If you are both the singer and songwriter you hit the jackpot because you receive all four royalties.

INCOME FROM ROYALTIES

Music lawyers and accountants spend years becoming experts in this complicated arena, so the following is little more than a very basic course in royalties.

Record Royalties

These royalties are paid by the record company to the singer and are based on the number of albums or singles sold. They are negotiated between your record company and your manager and are stipulated in your record contract. They usually amount to anything between 13 and 20 per cent of the wholesale price – known as the published price to dealer (PPD) – of a CD. A young solo act or pop band with no track record will get the lower percentage, while superstars with the negotiating power of U2 or Robbie Williams will get 25 per cent or more. Then you have Michael Jackson, who was widely rumoured to have scooped a 50 per cent deal with his record company!

The wholesale price of a CD is around £9, and can sometimes be even lower. However, to make our sums easier we will say the wholesale price is £10 and we have negotiated a royalties rate of 15 per cent. That means the artist gets £1.50 per album.

However, the artist doesn't receive the entire percentage deal. A whopping 25 per cent is deducted for packaging, and another 6 per cent is also often deducted at this stage for producers' fees. These deductions would result in the artist ending up with just over £1 per album. The usual income for a pop band or singer per album sale is therefore somewhere between £1 and £2, depending on the contract.

The royalties for singles only amount to about 4 per cent of the retail price after production costs, which is about 20p per single.

Mechanical Royalties

Just as the performer receives royalties from record sales, the songwriter also receives royalties from the record company for recording their songs on CD or other formats. Artists such as U2, Coldplay and The Corrs will earn these royalties along with the record royalties discussed above. This is because they are both the singers and the songwriters.

Acts such as Kylie and Westlife, who largely record other people's songs, don't get a share of this slice of the pie.

These royalties amount to approximately 8.5 per cent of the wholesale price of a record. So if an album is sold to the record stores for £10, the songwriter's share will be 85p. Of course, if the songwriter has a publisher and they have a 70/30 split, then the songwriter's share will dwindle to around 60p.

Justin Timberlake may record twelve songs on his album, with each song written by a different songwriter. In this case each songwriter gets paid their share of one-twelfth of the 85p, which is 7p per song on every album sold.

If Justin Timberlake hasn't written the song he's performing here, he is earning public performance royalties for the songwriter.

If you're U2, you don't have to share any of this money. They write their own albums and own their own publishing, so they receive the entire 85p earned in mechanical royalties for every album sold, on top of the £1–2 in record royalties.

The songwriter also receives 'mechanicals' if their song appears in a movie or advert. If a song features in a big TV ad or film in the UK, expect to be paid between £10,000 and £30,000. There's bigger money to be made in the US. U2 turned down £15 million for the use of their hit, 'Where The Streets Have No Name', in a major car advert in America several years ago.

These royalties are paid by the record company to collection organizations such as the MCPS (Mechanical Copyright Protection Society) and are then distributed to the songwriters and their publishers. See C for Collection Societies.

Broadcast and Public Performance Royalties for Songwriters

More royalties for songwriters (and their publishers), payable every time their music is played over the airwaves, in public or performed live. These royalties are also paid for the lifetime of the songwriter, and seventy years beyond.

A public performance of a song can take place on the radio, the TV, in movies, in nightclubs, on stage at a concert, or even as background music in your local hairdresser, restaurant or bar.

There are many different ways of collecting this money, monitoring what's being played and applying the appropriate fee or licence. There are set tariffs of £50 annually for a doctor's waiting room in which a radio is playing, for example. Radio stations pay a percentage of their advertising revenue, and the BBC pays according to its audience size.

When music is performed live, royalties must be paid to the songwriter. For example, when Westlife or any other band perform a concert, they must pay a 3.5 per cent tariff to the songwriter. This tariff is based on ticket sales. So, say 10,000 fans pay £25 each on the door and the ticket sales amount to a total of £250,000. The tariff of 3.5 per cent of £250,000 amounts to £8,125.

Westlife's tour manager, the promoter or the venue is obliged to submit a set-list of the songs that are performed during that show. This £8,125 fee is then divided between all the writers of the songs performed at that concert.

If you're a band like U2, performing your own songs, most of this money will come straight back into your pocket.

This money is collected by the PRS (Performing Right Society) in the UK, and IMRO in Ireland (Irish Music Rights Organization). See C for Collection Societies.

Airplay and Public Performance Royalties for Records

The record company and the performers on a CD are legally entitled to payment every time one of their CDs is broadcast on radio or TV, or played publicly in movies, bars, restaurants and shops. Singer-songwriters like U2 and Coldplay take a bite of this pie too, along with singers like Westlife. However, these royalties only last for fifty years after a sound recording is released.

Tariffs for airplay royalties are raised in many ways. They are charged according to the area size of a shop, the seating numbers in a restaurant, or the advertising income of a radio station. These royalties are monitored, collected and paid out by yet more collection agents: the PPL (Phonographic Performance Limited) in the UK and the PPI (Phonographic Performance Ireland) in Ireland. The money is split 50/50 between the record companies and the performers. (Note: the performers' income is collected by the PPI in Ireland, but is distributed to performers by the RAAP – Recorded Artists and Performers Limited.)

The PPL in the UK raised around £90 million for 40,000 performers last year, which amounts to £2,250 per head if it were distributed evenly. Of course, the superstars earn hundreds of thousands from these collection societies, while many lesser artists earn very little or nothing.

FAST TRACK TIP FOR THE CONFUSED

Still confused about music royalties? That's OK. Music accountants spend years learning this stuff. See C for Copyright and Collection Societies, and E for Earnings, and it will all become crystal clear. Maybe!

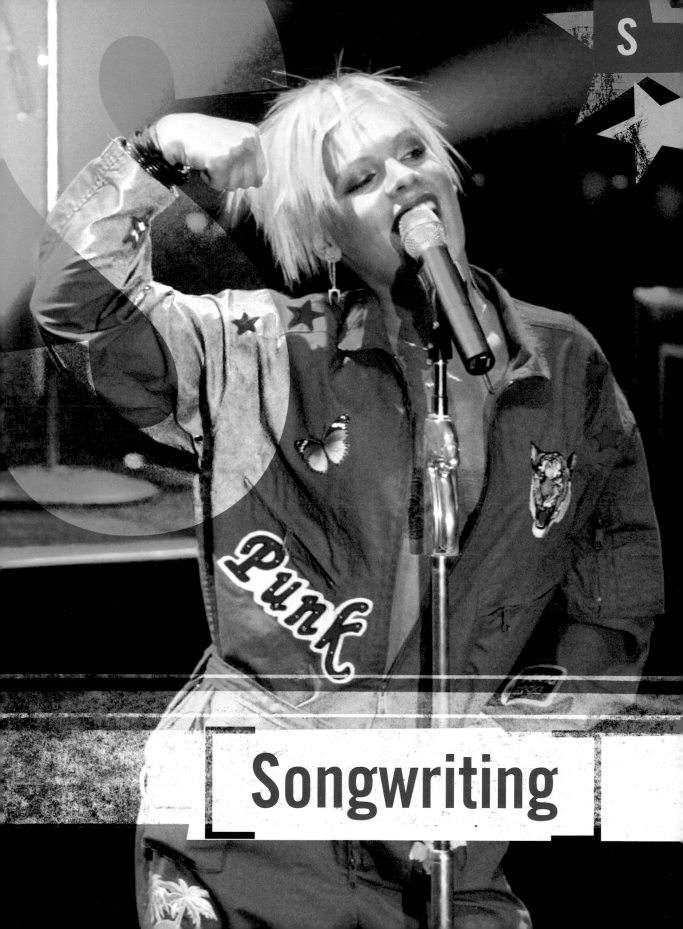

Songwriting

SONGWRITING
SO YOU'RE GONNA WRITE A CLASSIC?

When I stopped trying to write songs, that's when I'm able to begin writing songs. You have to just use your life and the things around you for your inspiration.

Lenny Kravitz

POP STARS SUCH as Jessica Simpson and Justin Timberlake are now writing songs as well as performing them – aren't they clever?

There's a mood these days that you're not a 'real' artist unless you're writing your own material. I don't subscribe to this belief. Frank Sinatra and Elvis Presley never troubled themselves with songwriting, and divas like Diana Ross, Aretha Franklin, Barbra Streisand and Cher have always left the songwriting up to the professionals. Even Michael Jackson had few songwriting credits on his earlier solo albums, including *Thriller*.

I prefer singers to just sing. Former *Pop Idol* runner-up Gareth Gates decided he wanted to write his own songs and look what happened. There's not many with the talent of Van Morrison, Bob Dylan, David Bowie, David Gray and Damien Rice. The songwriting should be left to the songwriters.

The sudden emergence of songwriting skills among pop stars is more to do with their clout in the music industry. Many songwriters will agree to give a writing credit to a major artist, knowing that the song will be a huge hit. So if you can't write your own music, don't despair. The record industry will make it look like you do anyway!

There're not many with the songwriting talent of David Gray.

If you can write songs, well done! This is a big bonus in the music world. The life span of a pop star or successful music artist can be very short, but songwriting is something you can do for ever.

And the real money in the music business is made from songwriters' royalties. You might remember that Westlife had a huge Number 1 hit with the song 'You Raise Me Up'. The real winners, however, were Irish songwriter Brendan Graham and Norwegian co-writer Rolf Lovland, who are estimated to have made more than £1 million from that song alone; it has already been recorded by more than 100 artists around the world.

THE FAST TRACK TO BETTER SONGWRITING

★ The Guild of International Songwriters and Composers provides services such as a free assessment of your music or lyrics. They offer advice on obtaining publishing deals, record deals, management deals, development deals, and can further advise on self-publishing and the self-release of records or videos. If you cannot write melodies or you cannot write lyrics, they can put you in touch with someone who can with their free collaboration service. The Guild publishes the magazine *Songwriting and Composing* for members.

Membership costs £48 for those in the UK and £55 for songwriters in Ireland. The Guild of International Songwriters and Composers is located at **Sovereign House, 12 Trewartha Road, Praa Sands, Penzance, Cornwall, TR20 9ST**. See **www.songwriters-guild.co.uk**; phone **(01736) 762826**.

★ The British Academy of Composers and Songwriters has a range of services for serious music writers who wish to develop and improve their careers. They offer free legal advice, regular magazines for members, and a programme of seminars and workshops that also provide social networking opportunities. In addition, they offer a collaboration service to link lyric writers with composers, or vice versa.

You can only become a full member of the Academy if you are a member of the PRS (Performing Right Society). However, you can become an associate member for £67.50. Full members include such luminaries as Bryan Ferry, Mick Hucknall, Robin Gibb and Mark Knopfler. The British Academy of Composers and Songwriters is located at **British Music House, 26 Berners Street, London WIT 3LR**. See **www.britishacademy.com**; phone **(020) 7636 2929**.

★ The BBC also has a useful website for budding songwriters called 'Sold on Song'. It provides lots of tips on improving your songwriting, as well as information on songs and their writers. See **www.bbc.co.uk/radio2/soldonsong**.

HOW DO YOU GET YOUR SONGS OUT THERE?

Ideally, you find a publisher who will sell your songs and even help you get a record deal. You may target specific music publishers and send them samples of your work. However, it's important to do your homework; it's a waste of time to send a dance track to a publisher that specializes in classical music. Unfortunately, many publishers no longer want to receive unsolicited material. See P for Publishers for more details.

You could also target your song at a specific artist or band that already has a record deal. Send your demo to the manager, publisher or to the artist themselves if you know them or know someone who does. Do make sure that the song is suitable for that particular artist and their genre of music.

Check out Songlink International, which is a resource for songwriters, A&R, music publishers, artists and managers. Unfortunately, it is a subscription service and costs £75 or €115 for three months, up to £240 or €359 for a year. This includes a monthly publication as well as online access. If you're not already a member of the PRS (Performing Right Society), you must send a sample demo of two of your best songs to join. Songlink International is located at **23 Belsize Crescent, London NW3 5QY**; or see **www.songlink.com**.

SONGWRITING SUPERSTARS

I deal with all the major publishers when I'm looking for songs, but I also deal personally with some songwriters.

Onc of America's most successful (and richest) songwriters, Diane Warren, owns her own publishing company, Realsongs. You'll know all her songs: 'I Don't Want to Miss a Thing' by Aerosmith; 'Because You Loved Me' by Celine Dion; 'Could I Have This Kiss For Ever' by Enrique Iglesias and Whitney Houston; 'How Do I Live?' by Trisha Yearwood; 'If I Could Turn Back Time' by Cher; 'Some Kind Of Miracle' by Kelly Clarkson; 'Unbreak My Heart' by Toni Braxton . . . I could go on and on. She has a real passion for music and for her songs. She still picks up the phone to call me and play her latest songs down the line. I love her because she's so passionate about her songs and is always trying to introduce her 'new babies'!

I also love veteran songwriter Albert Hammond. He co-wrote the huge Starship hit 'Nothing's Gonna Stop Us Now' with Diane, and also wrote and recorded the smash hits 'It Never Rains in Southern California' and 'The Free Electric Band'. Leo Sayer recorded 'When I Need You'; Whitney Houston made a hit of 'One Moment in Time'; and Julio Iglesias made a monster hit of his song, 'To All The Girls I Loved Before'.

Billy Steinberg is another great US songwriter who wrote 'Eternal Flame' for the Bangles and 'I Drove All Night' for Celine Dion and Roy Orbison. He and another writer, Tom Kelly, co-wrote a succession of hits, including Madonna's 'Like A Virgin', Cyndi Lauper's 'True Colours' and Chrissie Hynde's hit, 'I'll Stand By You'.

▶ Whitney Houston with my songwriting superstar pal, Diane Warren.

Talent Shows
Talent
Touring

T

TALENT SHOWS
STAND AND DELIVER

Rock monsters, Lordi, brought glory to Finland in the Eurovision of 2006 with their hit, Hard Rock Hallelujah.

X FACTOR SHRINKS IN comparison to the biggest, campest, greatest talent show spectacle in the world: The Eurovision Song Contest. This extravaganza was my first real experience of a talent show on a major scale. In 1980, my new twenty-four-year-old artist, Johnny Logan, represented Ireland with a song written by Shay Healy called 'What's Another Year?' This was Johnny's big chance. It was also mine and Shay Healy's. We were all broke and hungry for success. Shay said it for all of us when he wore a T-shirt which read: 'It is Imperative that I Win This Contest'. It was, and we did.

'What's Another Year?' sold more than half a million copies and reached number 1 in the UK charts. We thought we'd made it. Johnny was the dream artist – fabulous looks, voice and songwriting talent. However, behind the scenes he was embroiled in a messy contractual row with another manager and record company. It was the usual story: where there's a hit there's a writ. Within months, the promise of international stardom was over.

In 1984 I went back to the Eurovision Song Contest with another of my artists, Linda Martin. Linda, who remains one of my best friends, went out and performed Johnny Logan's song 'Terminal 3'. We came second. We were beaten by three brothers from Sweden singing 'Diggi-Loo, Diggi-Ley'.

By 1987 Johnny Logan's career was going nowhere. So he won the national contest in Ireland again and went to Eurovision with his own song, 'Hold Me Now'. Incredibly, he won for a second time.

Any normal person would be content with beating those kind of odds. Yet in 1992 Johnny wrote a song for Linda Martin called 'Why Me?' We won the national contest again and returned to the Eurovision Song Contest, which was in Malmo in Sweden this time.

Terry Wogan predicted that we were going to win. I didn't believe him. Now I shall forever bow to Sir Terry's infinite wisdom in these matters, because he was right.

Johnny and I don't have a bad Eurovision record between us – a total of three wins and one runner-up!

TALENT SHOW CRITICS

Talent shows were around long before *X Factor* and *American Idol*, and will continue to be around long after the demise of these TV shows. Yet they have been accused of having a bad influence on the music industry, and of not producing important or lasting musicians.

Kelly Clarkson is a world-class singer who might never have been discovered without *American Idol*.

It's not as if music talent shows are new phenomena – they were there in the era of the music hall, while *Opportunity Knocks* started on BBC radio way back in 1949. Yet critics commonly accuse talent show winners of lacking 'authenticity', 'integrity' or 'credibility'.

What's not authentic about Kelly Clarkson? She's a world-class singer who was discovered on *American Idol*. Clay Aiken is also enjoying a successful career. Where is the lack of 'integrity' in Shayne Ward? He'll be a major recording star for years to come, but I doubt he would ever have been discovered without *X Factor*. And is anyone telling me that *X Factor*'s Leona Lewis lacks credibility? She could become the UK's biggest international female star in years.

What about Girls Aloud, who were formed on *Popstars: The Rivals* in 2002 and are still going strong? Will Young is another talent show graduate who might never have been discovered without this massively popular TV genre.

203 ★

X FACTOR TERROR

Talent shows are a pressure cooker of stress and terror, and reality TV talent shows are the most terrifying of all. The schedule is horrendous, the work is non-stop and the pressure is huge.

Shayne Ward went into meltdown days before one of *X Factor*'s Saturday night shows. He just broke down sobbing, shaking and saying he couldn't go on during rehearsals.

We never saw it coming. It turned out that he couldn't deliver the Queen song 'Don't Stop Me Now'. It didn't suit him and his throat was bad that week. He hadn't said anything because he felt he was letting everyone down. Then, when he realized he couldn't do it, he buckled under the pressure.

On Friday morning we presented him with a new song, and less than twenty-four hours later he performed it flawlessly before a TV audience of nearly 10 million people.

My group Girls Aloud have had a major career thank to *Pop Stars: The Rivals* in 2002.

Talents shows like *X Factor* quickly separate the wheat from the chaff. It's easy to find people who can sing; it's a lot harder to find someone who can get out in front of an audience on live TV and perform under extreme pressure.

SHOULD I AUDITION FOR TALENT SHOWS?

It's terrifying. It can be demoralizing. So should you do it? Yes – if you have some talent and lots of drive and determination to succeed, then go for it.

Look at the winner and runner-up of the third series of *X Factor*. Both Leona Lewis and Ray Quinn entered and won local talent competitions before they auditioned for *X Factor*. The experience of performing under pressure was familiar to both of them.

If you believe you have talent and want to be a star, there are three things you need: experience, feedback and exposure. You can get all three by auditioning for talent shows.

Yes, auditions often involve a long and boring wait, but they are not a waste of time. You should use them as an opportunity to network with other like-minded people. Getting to know others who are also trying to make it in the business can be helpful. You can share contacts, experience and support.

Secondly, you gain experience from every audition. And with experience comes confidence. It doesn't matter if you get rejected; it's part and parcel of this business. Go for anything that gives you the opportunity to perform live. Get that experience, get that feedback and get the exposure you need to become a star.

For tips on auditioning see A for Auditions and X for X Factor.

NOT ALL IT'S CRACKED UP TO BE

> *Mick Jagger is the perfect rock star. There's nobody more perfect than Jagger. He's rude, he's ugly-attractive, he's brilliant. The Rolling Stones are the perfect rock group.*
>
> Elton John

DURING A PRESS interview, I was asked what I thought about Robbie Williams. I replied that I thought he was a karaoke singer, and I attributed much of his success to his former songwriter, Guy Chambers. Months later, as I was walking through the lobby of the Conrad Hotel in Chelsea, a very agitated Williams, who was surrounded by his entourage, confronted me. He stuck a tape recorder in my face and demanded that I repeat what I'd said in the interview. It was all very intimidating, but I did it – and I still stick by what I said. It was a very bizarre encounter – I thought for a minute I was going to get beaten up by Robbie Williams! He can dish out criticism, but it's clear that he doesn't like taking it.

Robbie Williams refuses to accept criticism.

Robbie has done fantastically well for the amount of talent he has. He's an amazing showman, but not an amazing singer. However, he surrounds himself with great talent in the form of writers, producers and video directors. Still, that encounter shows how remarkably insecure he is, despite having so much success. I still don't know why he got so upset by my remarks. Touchy guy, that Robbie.

TALENT, WHAT TALENT?

Robbie is living proof that you don't have to have a great voice or be a genuinely talented musician to become a music superstar. Robbie is simply very driven and ambitious and that's why he's a star. He's also a great entertainer who knows how to perform live. There are lots of people out there who are not enormously talented singers or musicians, but who have fared extremely well in the business. Talent helps, but it can be an overrated commodity.

Geri Halliwell, Victoria Beckham and even Kylie are examples of what bloody-minded ambition and hard work can achieve. I like Geri, and I worked with her and Pete Waterman on *Popstars: The Rivals* in 2002. However, like Victoria, she's not a real looker and she's not a singer. Yet they've both achieved an awful lot with very little. I love their ambition, even if it is blind ambition at times.

I also know Madonna has lots of fans, but I'm not one of them. Again, she wasn't overly blessed in the singing or looks departments, but you have to admire her because she's a triumph of ambition, focus and drive. Her determination for fame is a force to be reckoned with. She's also an incredible chameleon who manages to reinvent herself every few years. There are not many who would be brave enough to dance to 'Like a Virgin' at nearly fifty years of age. Let's hope she can withstand the pace for many years to come.

Britney Spears, Kylie Minogue and J Lo are others whose fame has outstripped their talent. They surround themselves on stage with troupes of dancers, million-pound sets and wardrobe assistants for dozens of costumes changes; they star in glossy videos that cost hundreds of

▶ Madonna: a triumph of ambition and hard work over talent.

thousands of pounds. And it all camouflages the fact that they're not naturally talented singers.

What Madonna, Britney, Kylie and J Lo *do* have, however, is star quality, that X factor. It's a blend of sex appeal, wit, warmth and vulnerability – the whole gamut of attractions. People are naturally drawn to them. The truth is, you can look like Miss World and sing like an angel, but if you don't connect with your audience you'll get nowhere.

They also have the brains to surround themselves with the best in the business, who make them look better. And more importantly they are ruthlessly ambitious, driven and hard-working – the basic ingredients for global fame and pop star success. It seems simple, but very few people have what it takes.

TOURING
ON THE ROAD AGAIN

BOYZONE'S FIRST BIG arena tour took place in the summer of 1996. There was a big set, fancy costume changes and expensive lighting. They played fifty dates in thirty-five different venues in front of 250,000 fans. The total cost of the tour was £2 million and the lads earned £20,000 each; it worked out at about £400 per concert. Keith Duffy probably earned a lot less, because he ran up a bar bill of £7,000 on one tour alone.

'We never paid any of our expenses at the hotels,' said Keith. 'Our tour manager, Mark Plunkett, used to do that for us. We did a small arena tour of just a few weeks and afterwards Mark said, "OK, lads, your bar bill for the tour came to sixteen thousand pounds." I said, "Ah, that's not too bad, that's about three grand each." But Mark said, "No, Keith, your share of the bill is seven grand." I didn't drink seven grand's worth of booze, but I was the f***ing eejit who was buying everyone else's drink!'

Boyzone may have earned £400 per concert in the early days, but they were also on a fixed wage of £700 a week. And their concert earnings doubled after the merchandising profits were divided. So they were hardly on the breadline. However, you can see that the margins can be tight, even on a successful sell-out tour.

Touring can be hugely lucrative, but only if tour costs are controlled with an iron fist. See C for Concerts to see how the takings can disappear.

FAST TRACK TO TOUR LOSSES

I'll let you in on a secret. Mick Jagger's boyishly skeletal frame is not only down to his high-energy performances on stage. When the Rolling Stones go on tour, one half of an entire articulated truck is devoted to transporting his running track. It's made of cork and is normally assembled in a marquee behind whichever stadium the rockers are performing in. He runs laps and laps around this thing for hours, apparently. Well, that's his way of coping with the stresses and rigours of touring.

Mick Jagger and his boyishly skeletal frame.

Legend also has it that Aerosmith's Steven Tyler took a chainsaw on tour so the band could wreck their hotel rooms more efficiently.

You can take the kitchen sink on tour, or you can smash the hotel one if you feel like it. You can demand the Presidential suite and bathe in bottles of champagne. You can do all of these things, as long as you realize that it's coming out of your own pocket. Big American bands have ended up millions of dollars in debt to their record company after a successful world tour, just because their expenses exceeded their income.

THE BIG GUNS

When Westlife went on tour in 2007, they moved everything in eight articulated trucks. When Justin Timberlake toured, it took twenty-two articulated trucks. And when Madonna went on tour the last time, she was accompanied by 100 articulated trucks.

At the top end of the music scale – the Rolling Stones, U2 and Paul McCartney – ticket sales are huge, but so too are the costs. The Rolling Stones' last outing, 'A Bigger Bang', was the biggest-ever grossing tour, racking up £219 million at the ticket office in 2006. U2's 'Vertigo' is the second-highest grossing tour of all time, earning £201 million after playing to an audience of 4,619,021.

However, the costs of huge amounts of equipment, cutting edge technology, roadies, transport, accommodation and high production values run into millions.

▶ Westlife travel lighter than most on tour.

CAN AN UNSIGNED ACT GO ON TOUR?

Touring is such an expensive prospect that it's really not an option for a new and unsigned act. The costs of transportation, accommodation and equipment are unlikely to be recouped from the proceeds of ticket sales. Some unsigned acts do tour successfully, but they tend to be veterans who had previous record contracts and chart hits. They usually have a lean touring machine, with minimal staff and an extensive national or international fan base.

ALWAYS THE BRIDESMAID, NEVER THE BRIDE

Many acts start out on the live gigging scene as the support act to a bigger band. In the past, record companies often paid £25,000 or £30,000 to buy a place on tour with a major act. Even though this is no longer the norm, touring as a support act remains an expensive prospect. The new act has to shell out for transportation, crew, accommodation and food. If it's still something you want to do, approach the act that you like, or their manager, and offer your services. I place unsigned or newly signed pop acts on tour with Westlife and Shayne Ward all the time.

THE TOUR ADVANCE

The record company can usually be persuaded to advance 'tour support' for their acts. A new act is not expected to cover the costs of a tour from ticket sales, so the advance is to supplement the losses that you are expected to make while touring.

An emerging act may expect to receive up to £50,000 from the record company. However, even though gigging is an important promotional tool for the record, this tour advance comes out of your pocket. It's not refundable, but it is recoupable, and will be deducted from any royalties by the record company.

SETTING UP A TOUR

So you're going on tour. The record company calls in the agent and the manager to discuss the length of the tour, the venues and the cities. Then the agent talks to promoters, checks out venue availability and sets up a rough schedule. The promoter takes a chance on what he's been assured is a hot new act. He books the venue and starts promoting the show. With a bit of luck, the tour will be laid out in an organized fashion; however, Boyzone often used to accuse me of throwing darts at the map, because they normally ended up on opposite sides of the country for every gig.

THE TOUR MANAGER

This is a completely different guy to the manager. He's an extra pair of hands on tour, looking after the logistics of getting the band from A to B and ensuring the artists get on and off the stage with the minimum amount of trouble. He supervises the stage rig, the PA system and the temper tantrums. With an emerging act, or even a medium-sized act, he can also be the driver, the doorman, the roadie and merchandise salesman. You can take it that your average tour manager has to deal with a lot of headaches from the artist, the public, the promoters and the manager. It's not the most enviable job in the business!

HOW TO RUIN A SUCCESSFUL GIG

On the final night of their 'Vertigo' tour in Australia, U2's legendary guitarist, The Edge, said, 'Thank you, Sydney' to 60,000 punters in Melbourne. The outraged audience booed in reply. He tried to save himself by saying, 'What I meant was, thank you, Sydney, Brisbane and Melbourne . . . but most of all Melbourne!' Too late. The damage was done.

Alanis Morissette was greeted by 15,000 screaming fans during her first gig in Peru a few years ago. They screamed even louder when Alanis ended with 'Thank you, Brazil!'

And Charlotte Church made the same gaffe a few years ago when she told her audience that she loved being in America. Her comments were met with a stony silence. She sang her song and quickly left the stage. Some time later she reappeared to make an announcement: 'Someone told me backstage that we're in Canada . . . I'm so sorry!'

It happens so often that it's a tour cliché. Still, don't do it. It really hacks off an audience. Do them the courtesy of memorizing where you are on a tour. Write it on the back of your hand if you have to. Or do as Westlife do. Kian Egan says: 'It's great to be able to shout "Thank you, Glasgow" or "Thank you, Dublin", but anytime we're ever in doubt we just shout "Thank you, everybody!" '

Justin Timberlake took twenty-two articulated trucks on tour.

U

Unions

UNIONS
YOU'LL NEVER WALK ALONE

[*All the world's a stage and I can't get an Equity card.*]

Anon

BUDDING SUPERSTARS CAN'T do it all alone. You'll need help and good advice if you are going to make a living in the music business. Unions are a very important source of support for self-employed musicians, bands, singers and performers, who might otherwise be open to exploitation.

MUSICIANS' UNION UK

The Musicians' Union in the UK is a great resource for music professionals. They have specialist officials tackling every kind of issue raised by their 32,000 musician members, and can also provide free legal assistance and a contract advisory service. They hold useful courses, seminars and workshops, which provide great networking opportunities for young hopefuls. The Union will also help you with salary and pay rate negotiations, and advise on partnership contracts for bands.

Their website contains a wealth of information and advice on everything from contracts to rehearsals and gig rates. They have several offices, in London, Cardiff, Birmingham, Manchester and Glasgow. Northern Irish artists are looked after in the Glasgow office.

Concessionary subscriptions for under-twenty-ones or under-twenty-fives on the New Deal scheme cost £54 per year or £4.50 per month by direct debit. The standard subscription is £120 annually or £9.67 per month for anyone earning below £15,000. The Musicians' Union is located at **1a Fentiman Road, London SW8 1LD**. See **www.musiciansunion.org.uk**; phone **(020) 7840 5504**.

EQUITY

This performers' and actors' union welcomes professional singers who work in choruses and groups, and individuals who work in pubs, clubs, concerts, opera, pop, theatre, recordings, sessions, radio, television and films. It produces a comprehensive guide to the minimum rates of pay for singers, available free of charge to any Equity member who requires it. It also produces a publication called *Singers' News*, which is sent out twice a year and is free to all those on the singers' register.

Equity is located at **London Office Guild House, Upper St Martins Lane, London WC2H 9EG**. See **www.equity.org.uk**; phone **(020) 7379 6000**.

MUSICIANS' UNION OF IRELAND

The Musicians' Union of Ireland was set up in 2003 as part of SIPTU (the Services, Industrial, Professional and Technical Union). They will look over their members' contracts, but they don't offer any free legal advice. Union subscription rates start at €1.90 per week and increase according to your earnings.

The Musicians Union of Ireland is located at Liberty Hall, Dublin. See **www.siptu. ie/musicians**; phone **(01) 858 6404**.

FIRST MUSIC CONTACT (IRELAND)

Although it's not a union, First Music Contact may be a better source of help for Irish artists. It offers free information and advice to artists at all levels of their careers. If you need help getting started or want someone to look at a contract, it can help.

First Music Contact is located at **Space 28, North Lotts, Dublin 1**; phone **(01) 878 2244**. You can book a free consultancy by emailing them at **info@firstmusiccontact.com**.

V

Venues
Videos
Vocals

THE RENT OF THE HALL

Showgirl Kylie knows how to put on a display in any venue.

CAN'T FIND A PROMOTER willing to stage your show? Become a DIY promoter *and* a superstar by hiring your favourite venue yourself – well, you can dream, right?

UK VENUES PER NIGHT	
Ministry of Sound:	£5,000
Shepherd's Bush Empire:	£10,000–12,000
Royal Albert Hall:	£30,000
SECC Glasgow:	£30,000
Odyssey Arena, Belfast:	£35,000
Wembley Arena:	£40,000
Manchester Evening News Arena:	£50,000

IRISH VENUES PER NIGHT	
The POD:	€5,000
Vicar Street:	€6,500
The Olympia Theatre:	€6,500
The Point:	€37,000
Croke Park:	€800,000–1 million

VIDEO KILLED THE RADIO STAR

> *A good video can make all the difference.*
>
> Brian May of Queen

MICHAEL JACKSON AND Janet Jackson's 1995 video for 'Scream' cost an incredible $7 million. This is a lot of money when you consider that most record companies charge the artist 50 per cent of the video's cost. Puff Daddy's 1998 video for 'Victory' is estimated as the second most expensive video of all time, costing $2.7 million. Christmas came early for the directors of these videos, as he or she normally receives 10 per cent of the budget.

The days of the bloated Hollywood video production are now largely in the past. Those videos were made in an era when MTV was the dominant player in the music business in the eighties and nineties. To break an artist or to have a hit record you needed lots of airplay from MTV, and you were only assured of airplay if you had a great video. This is no longer the case, as MTV is now more concerned with reality TV, and there are hundreds of new video music stations and music shows.

Rihanna's sexy Umbrella video helped catapult her to the top of the UK and Irish charts.

Incidentally, the first ever video that featured on MTV when it came on air in 1981 was the Buggles hit, 'Video Killed the Radio Star'.

Boyzone made their first video, 'Working My Way Back To You', for less than £2,500. The band wasn't signed and we had no budget. The director, Bill Hughes of Mind the Gap Films, is a friend of mine, and on the shoot he was the producer, art director, production designer, taxi driver and tea lady. He remembers collecting Ronan Keating and Stephen Gately on the cold winter morning we were doing the shoot. 'They looked more like sad little urchins than pop stars,' he says.

Their next video, for 'Love Me For A Reason', cost £4,000, and Bill managed to blag jumpers from designer Lainey Keogh and suits from John Rocha. It was shot in Dublin's

POD club, which is owned by Boyzone's co-manager John Reynolds. We even blagged the candles for the video. The single went to Number 2 in the UK and the video was played for two months solid on *Top of the Pops*. We've come a long way since then, with the average Westlife video costing between £100,000 and £200,000.

The video budget for a minor artist or emerging star would normally be £30,000 to £50,000. The big American music stars expect a budget of £200,000 or more. Big budget splurges do still occasionally happen: Janet Jackson's 2006 video for 'Call On Me' was estimated to have cost $1 million.

DO I NEED A VIDEO?

Not long ago I would have said there was no need for a struggling artist to go to the expense of producing their own video. These days I'd say, what's stopping you?

Digital wizardry in cameras and computers allow even rank amateurs to create affordable music videos. More importantly, there are countless ways of getting that video distributed to a potential worldwide audience for free. And it only takes one A&R, one talent scout or one person in the music business to see it and your life can be changed.

And there is no reason why amateur video should equate with bad video. Fatboy Slim had a huge hit with 'Praise You', thanks largely to the great (and cheaply shot) 'guerrilla-style' video by Spike Jonze.

The huge success of American rockers OK Go is largely down to their knack of producing oddball budget videos that have become 'viral' internet sensations. **The video for the track 'A Million Ways', which features the lads dancing around a back yard, was produced for less than $10.** Their entire budget was spent on the tape that they inserted into their borrowed camera. They even got the services of a choreographer for free because she's the sister of the lead singer.

▶ OK Go have mastered the art of making brilliant videos on the cheap.

> *Videos destroyed the vitality of rock and roll. Before that, music said, 'listen to me'. Now it says, 'look at me'.*
>
> Billy Joel

With more than 9 million hits to date, 'A Million Ways' is now officially the most downloaded video in music history. The clever follow-up video for their single 'Here It Goes Again' involved the use of several treadmills. The video was watched by 1 million people in six days on YouTube, and they performed the synchronized feat live at the MTV Awards in 2006. Watch OK Go and learn.

VIDEO PROS

If you really don't think you're up to shooting a video, consider saving up for a low-end professional production. There are video companies out there who will provide a broadcast-quality music video for £1,000 to £2,000. Check music publications for their adverts, but always ask for references and examples of previous work before you hand over your hard-earned cash and commit to immortalizing yourself on a music video.

FAST TRACK TO SHOWCASING YOUR VIDEO

Revver.com

Revver is a video site where you can actually make money from showing your video. Viewers see a short advert when they download a video from the site. Revenue from the ads is largely split 50/50 between the video creator and Revver. The site's biggest success story to date is not a music video, but a video based on the phenomenon of the cola geysers that erupt when you drop a mint Mentos into a bottle of Coke. 'Experiment Number 137' cost $300 and received 6 million views; it made $30,000 in viewings on Revver. (Search for 'Extreme Diet Coke' on the site.) The guys behind it have since made more cola-geyser videos, but the original 'Number 137' is still the best.

YouTube.com

More than 100 million videos are watched every day on the internet video site YouTube. The company's slogan is 'Broadcast Yourself', and it allows people to watch and share original videos worldwide on the web.

There are lots of other video-sharing sites, such as **iFilm.com**, **tv.blinx.com**, **video.google.com**, **video.yahoo.com**, **flickr.com**, **grouper.com** and **bolt.com**.

Social Network Sites

Put your videos on **MySpace.com** or get them up on your Bebo Bands page. **Xanga.com** is also a popular networking site for music fans and artists. **Purevolume.com** and **AbsolutePunk.net** are popular sites for American punk bands, who post free files for sampling.

FAST TRACK TIPS FOR SUCCESSFUL DIY VIDEO MAKING

Simplicity

You don't have to be Scorsese to make a perfectly good music video. Recording a live performance is probably the easiest thing to do. Set the camera relatively close in and capture the performance of the entire song without a break. Then just insert a few close-ups of guitar work or similar and you have a perfectly functional video.

Script It

If you want to do something more elaborate, script it out. Decide on the images you want for every bar of music. Sketch it out storyboard style – you don't need to be Michelangelo; stick figures will do.

Sound

It's best to use a recorded version of the song as the soundtrack for the video.

Serial Shooting

Shoot yourself performing the number several times from various camera angles. If you're shooting a band, focus on a different member for every performance.

Scene

Set the scene and get the mood right. If you're doing an upbeat pop song, don't record it in a dreary pub. Make sure the background to the video is complementary to the real star of this shoot – the music.

Style

Make sure the style of your video matches the music. You don't need frantic action if you're recording a romantic ballad. That will just distract you from the song. You also don't want long, lingering shots if you're producing a punk video.

Synchronizing

Some performers have come up with the idea of synchronizing their songs to existing sources of footage from TV or movies. Sadly, this is a copyright infringement. Steer clear of legal problems – don't do it.

Specialists

Go to professional video sites for free advice. See **www.musicvideowire.com** or **www.geniusDV.com**, which have technical advice on everything from making a budget video to streaming and compression.

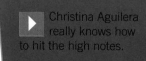
Christina Aguilera really knows how to hit the high notes.

HIT THOSE HIGH NOTES

My vocal style I haven't tried to copy from anyone. It just developed until it became the girlish whine it is today.

Robert Plant of Led Zeppelin

HOLLYWOOD ACTOR GEORGE Clooney spent three months rehearsing and receiving vocal coaching for the Coen brothers' movie, *O Brother, Where Art Thou?* He desperately wanted to perform the song 'I Am a Man of Constant Sorrow'. And because his aunt was the famous singer Rosemary Clooney, he thought he could carry it off. However, after his first session in the recording studio, he quickly realized that no one was enthusiastic about his performance skills and he admitted defeat. He claims the Coens had the real singer, Dan Tyminski, in the studio all along, ready to go.

And the moral of the story is: no amount of vocal coaching can turn a bad voice into a good one. Not even George Clooney's.

WILL VOCAL TRAINING HELP ME?

Before you even think about going for vocal training, you have to be honest about your natural singing ability. I'm constantly amazed by the number of people who appear before me in *X Factor* or other auditions, who are clearly astonished to be told they haven't a note in their heads. **Get a tape recorder or borrow a karaoke machine and actually record yourself singing.** Play it back and really listen and assess whether there is talent there. Let other people listen. If the answer is a resounding affirmative, then go and get professional singing lessons. Vocal coaching will help you to improve that talent and protect your voice.

HOW MUCH WILL A VOCAL COACH COST?

Private singing lessons can be expensive; expect to pay anything from £25 upwards per hour. The likes of David and Carrie Grant from *Fame Academy* charge up to £250 per hour. The fabulous Yvie Burnett charges a similar amount when she's working for record companies, but she's a softie when it comes to young singers, although you're still looking at £125 an hour for her time.

X Factor vocal coach Yvie Burnett with 2006 runner up Ray Quinn.

Finding the right singing teacher or vocal coach requires research. You could try shared classes, which are far less expensive; they will also enable you to see if the teacher suits you before committing to more expensive private lessons. Also, remember that it may be months before you begin to see any noticeable results.

FAST TRACK TO FINDING A VOCAL COACH

Check out **www.singing-teachers.co.uk/directory**, which has a list of teachers for every area of the UK, and also has listings in Dublin, Cork and Galway in Ireland.

Try the list provided by the Association of Teachers of Singing in the UK, which is available on **www.aotos.org.uk**. The Incorporated Society of Musicians also has a site that allows you to search for music teachers of all types, region by region in the UK, at **www.ism.org**.

You'll also find regional lists of vocal coaches at **www.musicteachers.co.uk** and **www. musiclessonsonline.co.uk**. Anyone in Ireland looking for vocal lessons should look up 'voice' on the site **www.learnmusic.info**. Many singing teachers can be found under 'music schools' at **www.yell.com** in the UK or **www.goldenpages.ie** in Ireland.

FAST TRACK TIP TO IMPROVING YOUR VOICE

See the top website for singers, singing teachers and students of voice at **www.vocalist.org.uk**. It has pages of voice training exercises and techniques, as well as other resources to improve your singing ability, and it's all available for free.

FAST TRACK TIP TO INSTANTLY IMPROVING YOUR VOICE!

Auto-Tune is a computer program that can make a voice sound perfectly in tune. Many regard it as a bit of a cheat. It's used to disguise a less-than-fabulous vocal, and is being employed more and more in the modern recording studio and during live shows. It can also provide that electronic voice effect that you hear in Cher's 'Believe' and 'Freak Like Me' by the Sugababes.

TOP VOCAL COACHES

Yvie Burnett

It is a pleasure to work with Yvie on *X Factor*. She gets the best out of people and really boosts their confidence at the same time. She did tremendous work with Shayne Ward, because he was not always the most confident performer. I met Yvie at the launch party for G4 after the first season of *X Factor*. I was introduced to her by her husband, Gordon Charlton, who is an A&R at Sony. I thought she would be perfect for the show, but the *X Factor* producers were against using an unknown at first. She turned out to be terrific and the contestants loved her. She has sung at the Royal Opera House in Covent Garden, but says she's still not convinced she could pull off a performance on *X Factor*. See **www.yvieburnett.com**.

Mark Hudson

American producer and songwriter Mark Hudson worked with Sharon Osbourne as the musical director and vocal coach for her *X Factor* contestants. This Grammy-award winner was a friend of the Osbournes long before *X Factor*; he says he's the son they never wanted. He's terrific, especially for rock singers, and has worked with Aerosmith, Bon Jovi, Cher and Celine Dion. He's a real eccentric, but he's also an example of a truly committed talent who worked miracles on the *X Factor* contestants.

David and Carrie Grant

David and Carrie from *Fame Academy* are great vocal coaches. In the past, David had a pop career with Linx, while Carrie sang at the Eurovision Song Contest when she was seventeen. They have worked with acts such as Take That, Will Young and Charlotte Church. They've also brought out their own vocal coaching book and DVD. See **www.carrieanddavidgrant.co.uk**.

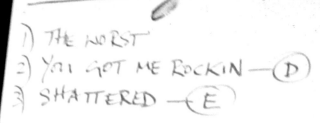

1) THE WORST
2) YOU GOT ME ROCKIN — Ⓓ
3) SHATTERED — Ⓔ

W

Websites

WEBSITES

USEFUL SITES ON THE PATH TO STARDOM

[
The internet is the most important single development in the history of human communication since the invention of call waiting.

Dave Barry
]

I'VE COMPILED A list of websites for music organizations, magazines and trade bodies, which those setting out in the music business may find useful. Some of these sites already feature in earlier chapters but contain so much of general interest and information that they're worth listing again. Other more specific interest websites, such as those for associations of producers, accountants and music lawyers, can be found in their relevant chapters.

Access to Music

Access to Music provides popular music education courses, training and consultancy in the music industry for all ages. The courses are free or heavily subsidized. See **www.accesstomusic.co.uk**.

BBC Blast

This site encourages younger students to get involved in the arts and music by providing opportunities, information and guidance. See **www.bbc.co.uk/blast**.

BBC 1 Music

This is a great resource for anyone who wants a career in the music industry. Industry experts give an insight into their jobs, and there's also information for bands and acts hoping to break into the industry. See **www.bbc.co.uk/radio/onemusic**.

Billboard

American trade magazine for the music business. See **www.billboard.com**.

British Academy of Composers and Songwriters

They have the largest composer and songwriter membership in the world, with over 3,000 UK music writers registered. See **www.britishacademy.com**.

British Music Information Centre

Offers resources for new classical music in the UK, as well as ethnic, pop and jazz music. See **www.bmic.co.uk**.

British Music Rights

Represents the copyright interests of composers, songwriters and publishers. See **www.bmr.org**.

British Phonographic Industry

Represents the record companies and organizes the annual Brit Awards. The site includes numerous music industry contact details. See **www.bpi.co.uk**.

Equity

This union is not just for actors; it also represents singers in the music business. See **www.equity.org.uk**.

Generator.org

Information for young people who want to embark on a career in the music industry. See **www.generator.org.uk**.

Guild of International Songwriters and Composers

Great advice and information on services for songwriters and composers around the world. See **www.songwriters-guild.co.uk**.

Making Music.org

Making Music represents amateur and semi-professional music groups and organizes training opportunities. See **www.makingmusic.org.uk**.

MCPS-PRS Alliance

These are separate societies, but work alongside each other. Both collect and distribute royalties for songwriters and composers. See **www.mcps-prs-alliance.co.uk**.

MIDEM

The trade fair of the music business. This international record, music publishing and video music market is held each year in Cannes in the south of France. See **www.midem.com**.

Music Education Directory

A useful site for anyone considering further education in music. Contains a list of 500 part-time and full-time courses and degrees in the UK and Ireland. See **www.bpi-med.co.uk**.

Music Indie.org

This is run by the Association of Independent Music, which supports independent record labels. It includes details of how to set up your own music label. See **www.musicindie.org**.

Music Managers' Forum

Represents managers and seeks to raise professional standards in music management. See **www.musicmanagersforum.co.uk**.

Music Manifesto

A practical guide for anyone wanting to add another string to their bow and considering a career in teaching music. See **www.musicmanifesto.co.uk**.

Music Tank

This is a free resource for music industry news, information and advice. It's run by the University of Westminster and aims to provide a business development one-stop shop for the UK music industry. See **www.musictank.co.uk**.

Musicians' Union

Useful website for those entering the music business; much of the content can be accessed by non-members. See **www.musiciansunion.org.uk**.

Music Week

This is the UK version of America's *Billboard*. It's a trade magazine for the UK music business, which also has a great directory that you can access online with free registration. See **www.musicweek.com**.

NUMU

Allows young people to showcase their music, meet others and learn new skills. It's designed to support the primary and secondary school curriculum. See **www.numu.org.uk**.

PPL (Phonographic Performance LTD)

Collects royalties for record companies and performers for the airplay and public performance of sound recordings and music videos. See **www.ppluk.com**.

Pro-Music

This site promotes legitimate online music services and is an alliance of musicians, performers, artists, record companies and music stores. See **www.pro-music.org**.

Soundgenerator.com

This site features music news, reviews and free musicians' directory. See **www.sound generator.com**.

Use Your Ears

A useful network for musicians – both signed and unsigned – and industry professionals. See **www.useyourears.co.uk**.

Vocalist.org

For singers, singing teachers, session singers and everything related to singing. See **www.vocalist.org.uk**.

Youth Music

This group supports music and training for everyone up to the age of eighteen. Events are held all over the UK. See **www.youthmusic.org.uk**.

WEBSITES

IRELAND
CPU
Ireland's largest independent music website. See **www.cpu.ie**.

First Music Contact
This umbrella group for music collectives is grant-aided by the Irish Arts Council and offers free advice and information for bands and artists at all levels. Book a free consultancy. See **www.firstmusiccontact.com**.

Hot Press
Irish music magazine, *Hot Press*, has a useful website with a good music directory, along with music news and reviews. However, there is an annual subscription of €20 to the site. See **www.hotpress.com**.

IMRO (Irish Music Rights Organization)
IMRO is the Irish version of the PRS in the UK. It collects and distributes royalties for songwriters and composers for the public performance of music on radio, concerts, etc. See **www.imro.ie**.

IRMA (Irish Recorded Music Association)
IRMA is the trade association for the record companies in Ireland, promoting and protecting the welfare of the Irish record industry. It's also involved in the Irish charts and hosts the annual IRMA awards. See **www.irma.ie**.

MCPS Ireland
This organization does the same as the MCPS in the UK. It collects money on behalf of singers, composers and publishers from recordings such as CDs, movies, etc. See **www.mcps.ie**.

Phonographic Performance Ireland (PPI)
Collects royalties for record companies and performers for the airplay and public performance of sound recordings and music videos. See **www.ppiltd.com**.

RAAP (Recorded Artists and Performers)
Distributes the monies raised by the PPI (see above) to Irish artists. See **www.raap.ie**.

X Factor

X FACTOR

SO YOU THINK YOU HAVE TH
X FACTOR?

> *I would never have been discovered without the X Factor. I was just doing the working men's clubs. I never expected to be noticed doing that, that's why I went for X Factor.*
>
> Shayne Ward

IT'S INCREDIBLE THE type of people who watch *X Factor*. I thought the actress Gwyneth Paltrow was pulling my leg when she told me she and her Coldplay husband, Chris Martin, never miss the show. They seem like such a, er, serious couple. Then I met her at the Prince's Trust Show and she turned out to be great fun. Gwyneth even gets her mum to tape the show for her when she's back in the United States!

THE *X FACTOR*

On Wednesday, 17 March 2007, I was in the Grand Hotel, Stockholm when I got a call from the executive producer of *X Factor*, Richard Holloway. It was around the time we were due to talk about renewing contracts for the show, so I was expecting his call. The last series had gone really well and the ratings were higher than ever, so I decided that I was going to play hardball and look for more money this time before I signed. Then Richard dropped the bombshell. He said he had bad news for me: I was off the show. I was devastated. Only a week earlier, I'd been sitting in Simon's house in Beverly Hills. We had talked about the fourth series and about bringing a fourth judge to the show. I'd urged Simon to consider the BBC's Chris Moyles. We'd also met up with Sharon Osbourne and had loads of laughs at Elton John's Oscar party. Throughout it all there was no indication that I was about to be booted off the show. In fact, Simon had even told me during the third season of *X Factor* that I would be doing the show as long as he was. So when I received that call from Richard Holloway, I had absolutely no inkling I was about to be canned.

I should make it clear that I wasn't upset about what was done – Simon and ITV have the right to hire and fire anyone they want – it was the way in which it was done. It was the fact that Simon didn't tell me himself. I felt like I'd been knifed in the back.

Presenter Kate Thornton was even more upset or, to be more exact, she was rip-roaring furious when she got a similar call from Richard Holloway. During the third series of *X Factor*, stories had appeared in the press claiming that Kate was about to get the axe. Simon pooh-poohed the whole thing both publicly and privately. In fact he personally assured her that her job was safe. As a freelance presenter, Kate had held her diary clear for six months of 2007 for a job that she thought was hers. She felt extremely

let down and hurt. Again, Simon didn't call her himself. She's better at sticking to her word than I am; she said she never wanted to talk to him again and she hasn't.

It wasn't as if Kate and I were being very naïve about doing the fourth series. The third series of X Factor had been the most successful one to date. We thought they would never try to fix something that wasn't broken, so we both felt completely shafted by Simon, even though he maintains it was nothing to do with him. He says it was ITV who demanded the changes in the line-up, and he was so wrapped up in *American Idol* at the time that he didn't think about it. Later he sent me a text saying how upset he was and that he regarded me as one of his closest friends. Well, I thought, if that's what he does to his friends, how does he treat his enemies?

I reacted to the news by throwing all the toys out of the pram. I told everyone I didn't want anything to do with him again. I said in the press: 'Never trust a man in heels.' Sharon Osbourne got into the fray and branded him 'a coward', which really annoyed him. Then there was a two-month cold war. At one point during that period I remember receiving another text from Simon telling me he was missing me 'a little'. I deleted it.

Gradually, of course, I cooled down. It's very hard to remain mad at Simon for long. I realized that I'd have to deal with Simon sooner or later and, to be honest, I did miss him a little bit. Bad as he can be, there's also a good side to him. Sometimes you just have to look hard for it. He's great fun to be around, but I recall someone very senior at ITV saying to me: 'Welcome to the world of Simon Cowell: population one.' That has always stuck with me. Also, I'd foolishly forgotten a very valuable bit of advice given to me by the great agent John Giddings: 'If you want loyalty in the music business, buy a dog.'

The first thaw in our cold war came when I got a call from Simon's long-suffering but gorgeous girlfriend Terri Seymour. In May I was on holiday in Miami and during our conversation he took the phone from Terri and we ended up making polite noises at each other and talked about Shayne Ward's new recordings.

Then, before I knew it, I was asked to appear on a *This is Your Life* tribute to Simon on ITV. Paula Abdul, the judge from *American Idol*, got the best line in the show: 'Simon is an egomaniac. He's the only man I know who screams his own name when having sex.

Simon Cowell, Sharon Osbourne and me – small parts of a big show.

And his idea of foreplay is staring at himself in the mirror.' That night I finally buried the hatchet with Simon rather than in him. We talked and laughed at a post-show party in Knightsbridge. He said that he thought it was a big mistake to fire me from the show. We were pals again, but at the same I never dreamt that I'd be offered my old job back.

In the meantime, American choreographer Brian Friedman, who had made his big TV début in the UK on Simon's ITV talent show, *Grease is the Word*, had been brought in to replace me on the show, and singer Dannii Minogue had been added as the fourth judge. By the time the *X Factor* auditions began in early June, I'd put the show behind me. I had other TV offers and was gearing up for the launch of new album releases by Shayne Ward and Westlife as well as the re-launch of Boyzone.

I'm not going to lie and say I didn't enjoy it when I started to hear that the new *X Factor* auditions were not going as well as ITV and Simon had hoped. Both Simon and Sharon sent me texts from the London auditions saying it wasn't the same and that they missed me. Sharon gave me the low-down and told me that the auditions lacked the old chemistry and the fun that we had. Other people around the show rang me and told me the sparkle was missing. I couldn't have been happier. Serves them all right, I harrumphed to myself. I was really astonished when I first heard word that there were plans in motion to get me back on the show. I don't really know what went on behind the scenes, but a few weeks later I got the official phone call from Richard Holloway on Thursday, 21 June, three months and two weeks after he fired me. He said that they wanted me back on the show for the Manchester auditions the following Monday. Needless to say, I was there. So, all is forgiven. Until they try to fire me again.

THE JUDGES

Back in 2004 when Simon Cowell rang me from LA to tell me that he was thinking of asking Sharon Osbourne to be the third judge on his new ITV show, *X Factor*, I was stunned. If there was one show that I couldn't stand, it was MTV's *The Osbournes*. If there was any member of the Osbourne clan that I disliked more than the rest, it was Sharon.

Originally, I'd heard that the *X Factor* line-up was also going to include top pop producer Pete Waterman. I wasn't exactly thrilled at the prospect.

Stock, Aitken and Waterman were one of the most successful songwriting and producing partnerships of all time, scoring more than 200 hits in the mid-eighties to early nineties.

I had already worked with Pete on the ITV show *Popstars: The Rivals* in December 2002. Pete, Geri Halliwell and I were judges on the series and his boyband, One True Voice, lost out in the end to my act, Girls Aloud. We traded a few insults in the media after the series concluded. I thought he was being a sore loser. He thought I was gloating. He took it all to heart and he didn't talk to me for years.

I like Pete but he picked the wrong songs and One True Voice never stood a chance. They disbanded soon afterwards. He should have just held up his hands and admitted it was his fault. Instead he was annoyed with me.

So things were bound to be really awkward if we were thrown together again on *X Factor*. Then all of a sudden Simon came up with the idea of recruiting Sharon Osbourne. At the time I would have preferred Pete Waterman, even if we weren't talking.

▶ Sharon Osbourne picking on me again!

Sharon

Sharon and I had some previous history. She was furious with me because I'd described her daughter Kelly as 'talentless' in a few interviews; she had even pulled Kelly out of a big pop charity show in Dublin because I was involved. I didn't like *The Osbournes* show. I didn't get her. I didn't get them.

So you'll gather that I wasn't looking forward to meeting the formidable Mrs O. I hoped that Simon would be an ice-breaker, if not a buffer between the pair of us on the first morning that we met for *X Factor* duty.

Of course, Simon was nowhere to be seen that morning.

So we were forced to bare our teeth at each other and exchange cautious pleasantries. Still, it didn't take long for me to realize that Sharon wasn't quite the witch I was expecting. I was surprised to discover that she's actually a charming and funny woman. If she held a grudge for what I'd said about her daughter, she hid it well. Now we're the best of pals, and she's an ally when Simon occasionally loses control of himself and is more pompous than usual.

Sharon is actually incredibly energetic, caring and really hardworking. She's also very shrewd. It's easy to see why Ozzy is such a success story.

Of course, the music business is in her blood. Her dad was the famous manager, Don Arden, who died in July 2007. He was the legend behind successful acts such as ELO, Gene Vincent, Ozzy and Black Sabbath. She was a stage-school diva before opting to work for her dad. There's very little Sharon doesn't know about the music business, and she also has a really good appreciation of all music genres.

Most of all, though, she loves her family and her yappy little dogs. And beware, because this tiny tornado is hugely protective of both. During an ad break in the third series of *X Factor*, celebrities in the audience were invited to ask the judges questions. Chris Tarrant poked fun at Ozzy: 'Your husband's very articulate, isn't he,' he remarked to Sharon. Big mistake. She hit the roof and called him a string of names that would make a sailor blush. The audience watched, bug-eyed and gobsmacked. By the time we went back on air, I was still shaking with shock.

Of course, everything hasn't always been rosy between us. She could have killed me when she chucked a glass of water over me during the second series of *X Factor*. The water also hit my monitor, which started sparking before it short-circuited and blew out. I might have been electrocuted during the live show. There's only so much I'll do for TV ratings, so now we have an understanding: if she ever does it again, I'll walk and I'll take her hair extensions with me.

Simon

I knew Simon for many years prior to *X Factor*. I first heard about him when he was establishing a reputation in BMG, signing successful acts like Sinitta, Sonia, 5ive and Robson and Jerome, and I finally met him for the first time at an Irish TV show called *Kenny Live*. He was there with Robson and Jerome, and I was there with Boyzone. We talked, and we agreed that we'd work on something together.

He ended up signing Westlife to BMG in 1998.

Unfortunately, he took an immediate dislike to Shane Filan, and wanted him dropped from the line-up, insisting that he didn't look right for the band. There was no way I wanted to lose a talented singer like Shane. He's the backbone of the group, and technically the best singer I've ever worked with. He's never, ever out of tune.

Yet Simon was adamant he had to go, and when he makes up his mind, there's nothing you can do to change it. So you just have to fool him. I told Shane he had to dye his hair for the band's final showcase in Dublin. Simon didn't even notice that the new blond guy was in fact the same band member he wanted replaced.

▶ Sometimes I'm forced to drastic measures because Simon Cowell just refuses to listen!

One of the biggest contradictions between Simon Cowell's public and private persona is his 'Mr Nasty' image. He revels in his conceited and acerbic public image, but in reality you'll never find a more polite and pleasant man. I've never seen him being rude to anybody off-camera; he has impeccable manners, whether he is dealing with a waiter in a restaurant or a chart-topping pop star. His mother, Julie, has reared him well.

He also has a soft side where animals are concerned, and is a big supporter of People for the Ethical Treatment of Animals. He hasn't actually got a pet because his lifestyle is crazy and his houses are like modern art galleries, but he's almost as kind-hearted as our own Dr Dolittle, Sharon Osbourne.

He was genuinely horrified to discover *Lord of the Dance* star Michael Flatley enjoys going big game hunting in Africa, and has a whole room in his manor in Castlehyde in Cork devoted to his safaris. Few would believe how incensed Simon was to hear that people would actually pay money to shoot animals for sport. Yes, he has a heart. He just hides it well.

He's also incredibly knowledgeable about the music business, and about television and marketing. He has an unerring instinct for a hit song – at least he always knows one when I bring it to him.

THE ROWS

The three of us get on famously at the audition stage of each *X Factor* season. However, as soon as the live shows start, everything changes and egos take over. The problem is that the three of us want to win. The stress levels soar as the show progresses.

I walked out in the middle of the second series of *X Factor*. Popular opinion is that the whole thing was a publicity stunt. It wasn't. I'd just received the second of two glasses of water in my face, courtesy of Sharon. I'd taken serious abuse from Simon, and had nearly been lynched by the audience for sending singer Maria Lawson home in favour of the Irish act, The Conway Sisters.

But the straw that broke the camel's back was seeing Simon Cowell on a TV chat show claiming I wasn't capable of judging a hamster competition. I just saw red. First and foremost, I'm a manager. *X Factor* is not my day job – it's a bit of mania that I get involved in for a small part of the year. That's when I decided he'd gone too far.

I wasn't going to let him destroy my professional reputation as a manager, so I threw the mother of all tantrums. I told Simon very precisely where he could stick his show and took the next flight back to my home in Dublin. I wouldn't take his calls, so he sent texts apologizing and telling me he was sorry and that he regarded me as one of his best friends. It was days before I put away my huff and returned in time for the following week's show.

Yes, there are times when I feel totally overshadowed by the two larger-than-life divas beside me. It's how Florence Ballard must have felt in The Supremes! However, my usual game plan is to let the other two create a lot of hot air while I concentrate on creating a winning pop act.

THE CONTESTANTS

From the moment Shayne Ward walked into the Manchester auditions and started to sing the Elton John song 'Sacrifice', I knew he had the X factor. Shayne had taken the day off from his job as a shoe salesman in the nearby Arndale Centre to audition for the second series. If he hadn't, he might still be selling shoes today. Now, he's on the path to becoming a music megastar.

By the time I saw Shayne in Manchester in the summer of 2005, I'd seen thousands of young hopefuls in auditions, yet I'd never seen anyone with so much instant star potential as Shayne Ward. My fellow judges, Simon Cowell and Sharon Osbourne, didn't miss his X factor either. There was no hesitation. All three of us voted him through.

When I discovered I was managing the under-25s for that series, I started telling people I already had the winner in my group. That was probably a mistake, because the word spread and Shayne became the bookies' favourite from the start! Yet I knew right from the beginning that he had the raw talent, the looks and image for pop stardom. But I still needed to know that he had the right attitude before I'd agree to manage him.

I won't manage anyone unless I believe in them and get on with them off stage as well as on. I will give artists 100 per cent as long as they give it back, but I won't deal with anyone, no matter how talented they are, if they have the wrong attitude. The contestants on X Factor are always on their best behaviour around the three judges – we hold their passport to the finals, and possibly to pop fame and fortune – however, some of them are not quite so helpful and humble when our backs are turned. They don't seem to realize that everything gets back to us, and we quickly hear about the divas who won't take instruction and the lazy slobs who aren't putting in the effort. This time, no one behind the scenes had a bad word to say about Shayne. He was pleasant to everyone and eager to work and to learn.

As the show progressed, I realized he was the whole package, and I knew he was a person I could work with. If I'm completely honest, I don't expect to find another Shayne Ward or another act with the same star potential on X Factor again. It would be fantastic, but I think he's one in a million. I believe he will become one of the biggest pop stars out there.

So what exactly is the X factor? It's that indefinable, unknown element that separates a good performer from a truly great one. It doesn't necessarily mean that he or she is more talented than another performer, only that he or she has something intrinsically more appealing.

I think Gareth Gates – the runner-up in the first series of *Pop Idol* in 2002 – was one of the few reality talent show finalists with real X factor. He had all the makings of a great British pop act. It's incredible that this guy could sing like an angel but could hardly speak at all. His stammer had got so bad that he communicated by writing in a notebook.

After a charity concert in Dublin I suggested that he should record the Barry Manilow hit 'Mandy' for his next single. He thought it was way too cheesy. So I got Westlife to record it instead and it became their twelfth Number 1 single in the UK.

I also ended up in the middle of what was probably one of the last meetings between Gareth and his former BMG record boss, Simon Cowell. I remember the meeting consisted of Simon talking a lot and Gareth holding up a sign saying 'I don't agree' a lot. Give me record sales and popularity over 'credibility' any day but Gareth wanted to be Justin Timberlake and there is only one Justin Timberlake. I hope he's successful in his comeback in 2007 because it would be a shame if he slipped through the net again.

Winning or losing TV talent shows is no guarantee of either success or failure. The band Hearsay, who emerged triumphant on *Popstars* in 2000, have long since disappeared. The so-called 'flopstars' from the same show, Liberty X, enjoyed a much more successful career. Similarly, Jennifer Hudson only reached seventh place on *American Idol* in 2004. Now she's the Oscar-winning diva from the movie *Dreamgirls* with a huge future ahead of her.

Girls Aloud, who were formed on *Popstars: The Rivals*, and Will Young from *Pop Idol* 2002 went from strength to strength after their wins. However, Michelle McManus, who won the second series of *Pop Idol* in 2003, is now more famous for losing weight than for her record sales.

The first series of *X Factor* was won by Steve Brookstein, thanks in part to Sharon Osbourne, who called him 'a fake' on national TV. I believe she provoked a massive sympathy vote which helped him win the show. What the audience didn't know was that she had had a row with him during rehearsals and was still furious. Anyway, where is Steve Brookstein today? I never liked him either and thought he was just another 'good singer' with no real star quality. There's a reward out for anyone who can find him now.

Meanwhile, my act, G4, who were the runners-up on the show, ended up the real winners. They released three hit albums and enjoyed a great career until June 2007 when they split up because they just weren't getting on with each other any more.

I never, ever thought Ray Quinn would reach the finals of the third series of *X Factor*. I think he's a great little worker, he's very professional and I think he's destined for West End stardom, but I just don't see him becoming a big recording artist.

The future of Leona Lewis is a hard one to call. She's a great singing talent, and she

should go stellar. But I don't know if she has the naked ambition, hunger and drive that's needed to be successful. There's not much star quality about her either just yet although she has the vocal ability in the studio where it counts. She's a bit too shy and a bit too normal. Still, J Records boss, Clive Davis, wants to work with her in the US, and if anyone can give her the star quality she needs, it's Clive.

THE *X FACTOR* AUDITIONS

A total of 5,000 hopefuls auditioned for the *Popstars* series in 2000. By the time the first series of *X Factor* came around in 2004, more than 50,000 showed up for the auditions. That rose to 75,000 for the second series in 2005. During the third series, 100,000 pop star wannabes were put through their paces and 15,000 turned up for one open audition, held at Old Trafford Football Stadum in Manchester, alone. The fourth series saw another 100,000 trying to make it through, and the programme had trouble limiting the

▶ Shayne Ward singing his way to success on *X Factor*.

final open audition at Birmingham's Alexander Stadium to 7,500 in July 2007. So it's hardly surprising that not everyone goes home happy. Many take it badly when they're advised to stick to the day job.

We invariably hear comments like 'Who the hell do you think you are, anyway?' Many deluded young people come to auditions and expect me, Simon and Sharon to say the same things their mothers tell them: that they're brilliant and there's no one else like them. Unfortunately, mothers and friends are not always the most reliable judges of talent.

The best advice I can give on auditions is to learn from the mistakes of others. You won't live long enough to make them all yourself, but a huge number of people seem determined to try. They see the mistakes that people made during previous auditions, and still come in the following year and repeat them. See A for Auditions.

Also, if you can't take a knock-back, don't show up. It's no good whinging when you get advice you don't want to hear from people who know what they're talking about. And remember, just because you didn't set the world on fire this time, it doesn't mean you never will. It was third time lucky for Shayne Ward when he auditioned for *X Factor* in 2005.

Simon, Sharon and I have been around the block a few times in the music business. We've paid our dues. We're not out to hurt anyone deliberately, but sometimes the truth is hard to handle. Please learn to take rejection. It's free.

The Yoko Ono Factor

THE YOKO ONO FACTOR

ACTRESS GWYNETH PALTROW has taken the smart route concerning her husband Chris Martin's Coldplay career. She steers clear of it. Gwyneth can sing, and even performed in the movie *Duets*, but she's insisted that she'll never do a duet with Chris. She says she's scared of becoming his 'Yoko Ono', so stays well away from the business of the band.

Outside interference has probably scuttled more bands than anything else. It's the age-old rock 'n' roll story: the band's going great until the singer's new girlfriend sticks her oar in.

The 'Yoko factor' refers to Yoko Ono's relationship with John Lennon. Yoko was widely blamed for the band's split because John broke the Beatles' longstanding no-wives-or-girlfriends rule and started bringing her into recording sessions. Her constant presence is said to have contributed to the growing tensions in the band.

Gwyneth Paltrow stays well away from the career of her Coldplay husband, Chris Martin.

Boyzone's Keith Duffy has referred to the 'Yoko Onos' who he claimed helped split up Boyzone at the height of their success. The truth is the band was already falling apart. I regularly took calls from the far side of the world, where one was complaining that another had a bigger room or that so-and-so was getting preferential treatment. Partners were just something extra to complain about.

Outside interference is not all about wives and girlfriends. Husbands and boyfriends cause just as many problems, as do mothers and fathers who won't cut the apron strings. Other individuals around the artists, such as stylists and tour managers, as well as rival business interests, can also cause issues. The real

problems begin when artists start to believe the whispers of 'you're a better singer than him, you should be doing lead vocals' or 'you're better than them, they're just riding on your coat-tails'.

Another problem is that many partners see a famous pop star lover as their own route to fame. These celebrity klingons are fonder of the limelight than they are of their partner. They become celebrities-by-proxy, and then use every opportunity to promote themselves and their 'career'. I prefer things the old-fashioned way. Back in the sixties, a pop star never had a girlfriend or wife, or if he did, she was kept firmly in the background.

> Nicky Byrne is proud of his family but they never interfere with Westlife. Here he is with his wife, Georgina, their baby twins, Rocco and Jay, and proud granddad and Taoiseach of Ireland, Bertie Ahern.

Fans also resent the 'significant others' in their heroes' lives; Linda McCartney was hated by Beatles fans.

One of the reasons why Westlife have survived and succeeded for so long is that they have never allowed anyone to interfere with the band. For many years no one knew of the existence of Shane Filan's girlfriend, Gillian, who is now his wife. She was perfectly happy to stay in the background. Everyone knew Nicky Byrne had a girlfriend because she was more famous than he was when the band started out. Georgina, now his wife, is the daughter of the Irish Prime Minister, Bertie Ahern, and is another Westlife wife who had no interest in elbowing her way into the limelight. Kian Egan has also been lucky in love with actress Jodi Albert. She had her own showbiz career long before she met Kian.

The only sure way to avoid significant others causing conflict in a band is to keep them well away from it. Ideally, bands should make a rule that family and partners do not tour with the band, that they don't appear backstage, and that they don't have a say in the band's business.

If you do come across an interfering outsider, tell them they're fired. They say, 'You can't fire me, I'm not in the band.' You reply, 'Exactly, so mind your own business.'

Z-List to A-List

THE MUSIC PROS' FAST TRACK TIPS TO THE TOP

LOUIS WALSH'S
TOP TEN TIPS FOR THE TOP

[1] Number one is always the song. If the song isn't right, nothing else will be; if the song is great, you're halfway to a hit. Throw in good promotion, radio play, TV play and record signings, and you have the right formula for a hit.

[2] Endless drive, ambition and the capacity for hard work are what lie at the heart of every successful artist. If you're a lazy person, don't waste your time. You only get out of this business what you put in. Music success demands sacrifice, discipline and self-denial.

[3] Perform live as often as you can. You need experience, feedback and exposure to learn to become a star. Live performance allows you to develop your stagecraft and your confidence.

[4] Meeting someone personally is worth a hundred phone calls. Get out and circulate in the right places, particularly at music industry events. Then work your way through the room – don't just focus on the chairman of the record company. The receptionist is a useful ally to have in your corner as well.

Me in a good mood.

[5] Never stop being a fan and never stop loving the music. Don't be afraid to admire other artists and their achievements. Listen, learn and stay on top of everything that is going on in music. Learn from the stars – read music biographies and autobiographies and see how they also started at the bottom!

I won't be happy until I am as famous as God.
Madonna

[6] Connect with your audience and your fans both on and off stage. That's what real star quality is all about. Be accessible to fans after concerts and on your website. Give them time and respect, and ensure you keep building your fan base rather than alienating it.

[7] Listen and learn. You may be a natural performer, but don't be a big mouth; there's a reason we all have two ears and one mouth. If you're clued into the business, you will learn who the best people are in every area and you will try and work with them.

[8] Hand out the fliers, send out the demos, sign the records, tour every huckster store, put up the posters, perform live and audition every chance you get: promote, promote, promote.

[9] Learn about the business side of things. See C for Collection Societies and Copyright for a start. Or do what I do and hire really good lawyers and accountants.

[10] I don't care if it's a cliché, this one is important: be nice to people on the way up, because you'll meet them all on the way down again. The music world is too small for anyone to act like an idiot and expect to get away with it.

COLIN BARLOW
HEAD OF POLYDOR RECORDS

Colin is the joint managing director of Polydor Records, which is the UK's flagship label and the market leader. When he was Polydor's top A&R, he signed Boyzone, Girls Aloud, Ronan Keating and Samantha Mumba.

'The key to getting signed is entrepreneurship. You have to get out there and get a buzz going. Spin is really important and that's where Louis Walsh is really good. He is the master of spin. Really, it's important because perception is nine-tenths of the law. If you can make people feel you're the hottest new thing around, the next big thing, you're already on the way there. You have to be clever and manipulate the hype. After that, you need general talent to back it up and you need a manager like Louis to get you the best deal.

'Any new artist has to set out and create a buzz about them. Don't wait for the record companies to do it for you. If you already have the hype behind you, you're in a position of strength when it comes to meeting with the record companies. Get yourself into the music magazines, style magazines, MySpace – the internet is the lifeblood of talent scouts today. Word of mouth is also important among DJs, producers, etc. Get out there and get people talking.

'I remember when Louis was looking to get Samantha Mumba a deal, she was everywhere. Anytime there was a Boyzone party, Louis had Samantha there. Anytime there was a Polydor meeting, Samantha would suddenly appear. Anywhere we were, she was there. There was no way we were going to be able to ignore her. So we signed her – yes, there was more to it than that, but you know what I mean.'

YVIE BURNETT
X FACTOR VOCAL COACH

Yvie is a classically trained singer who has performed at Glyndebourne. She has also worked wonders with X Factor stars, including Shayne Ward and Leona Lewis.

Vocal coach Yvie Burnett working her magic with Leona Lewis for *X Factor*.

'It's a false economy not to save up and spend money on a few singing lessons. Not only do you risk doing damage to your voice early on, but you are missing out on something that can make a valuable and noticeable improvement to your voice. Vocal lessons can make a huge difference and can ensure that your voice, which is your most valuable asset as a singer, is both protected and improved. It drives me mad when I hear young people say they can't afford singing lessons, but they have no problem spending money on highlights, false nails and sunbeds. Forget the hair extensions, the tanning sprays and the designer jeans. Instead, make the best of what is really essential to your career – your voice. It's very foolish not to.'

Kian Egan of Westlife.

GARY KAVANAGH
STYLIST

Celebrity snipper Gary Kavanagh, who works with the Peter Mark hairdressing chain in Ireland, has styled hundreds of stars, including Kylie Minogue, Celine Dion, Shayne Ward, Westlife and S Club 7. Kylie was so happy with her 'do', she went clubbing with him to Lillie's Bordello afterwards!

'Don't be afraid of change – all the big stars experiment with their image and reinvent their looks all the time. And let the professionals get on with their jobs. We're there to make you look good. There's nothing worse than someone who's on the defensive. Hair, make-up artists, stylists – we're all working to make you look better. If you have a specific look in mind, there's nothing wrong with bringing along photos or cuttings from magazines. Before I do a celebrity's hair I research all their various looks. When I did Kylie's hair I found a whole lot of different photos. She's always changing her image. I laid out all the photos in front of her and said, "OK, which Kylie do you want to be today?" '

KIAN EGAN
FROM WESTLIFE'S TIPS FOR THE TOP

★ Treat people the way you want to be treated yourself. Have respect for everyone and everyone else's job.

★ Never believe the publicity about yourself. We've seen acts who have let it go to their heads. They never last long.

★ Take advice from people in the music business who have been in it a lot longer than you. Never believe you know it all. We're lucky that we've been given some of the best advice in the business, and that we've taken it.

★ Work hard and do it right or don't bother at all. Learn your trade. Preparation and hard work are necessary. Take music lessons, dance lessons – anything that can improve or enhance your chances in the music world. If you work hard, success follows.

★ Earn a reputation for putting on a great live show. Make it the best it can possibly be. Again, preparation and rehearsal are the essential ingredients.

★ Fans are for life, as long as you look after them. Never take them for granted.

★ Believe in yourself – in the face of constant rejection, you're going to need self-belief and persistence.

★ Go into the music business for the love of music. Then learn the business side.

★ Don't forget to enjoy yourself, and don't take it all too seriously – if you're not enjoying yourself, you're in the wrong business.

PRISCILLA SAMUELS
CHOREOGRAPHER

Priscilla trains Westlife and Shayne Ward, and has worked with dozens of artists, including the Spice Girls, Tina Turner and S Club 7.

'Dance is so important to your overall performance if you want to be a pop star. Watch the artists you admire. Watch their steps and then get in front of the bedroom mirror and practise, practise, practise until you can do it too. Remember they will have gone through hours and hours of training, so you will too if you want to make it look easy.

'If you want to learn more, take classes. Don't just take any class. You wouldn't buy clothes without trying them on for size first, so don't pay for lessons until you know what you're getting. Watch the teacher in the studio taking class. See if what he or she is teaching is what you want to learn. Try lots of different dance forms and find out what you really like to do. You don't have to attend any fancy dance schools to be a good dancer. I didn't. You just have to have a real passion for it and the discipline to put in hours of practice.'

PAUL KRAMER
MUSIC JOURNALIST ON HIT SHEET

Paul runs this subscription industry music magazine, which appears on the desks of A&Rs and those in radio stations twice a month. It's a magazine that is taken seriously by all the professionals in the business. Subscription is £175 a year.

'We like to champion unsigned acts. We get around one hundred demos a week from unsigned acts, we listen to them and then we pick the best tracks and we feature them on a CD that goes out with the magazine every fortnight. It's taken seriously by A&Rs and we've had a lot of success. We helped break acts or made the first recordings of acts such as Mika, Corinne Bailey Rae, Gary Jewels, Aqua Lung and The Killers. Then we also hold a *Hit Sheet* Showcase once a month that gets a lot of A&R interest. I'm just looking to hear a great demo, but the hit rate is about two to five per cent, and you have to go through a lot of rubbish before you find the good stuff. If you have a demo that you think is really good, we want to hear it.'

KEITH DUFFY
OF BOYZONE

Keith has not only enjoyed a pop career, he has branched out into acting and made his mark on top TV shows including Coronation Street.

'People starting out in the business will hear a lot of advice. For me, it's really simple: just make a conscious effort to be nice and polite to everyone around you. Not in a false way, but sincerely. Just treat everyone how you'd like to be treated. There's that saying "be nice to everyone on the way up because you'll meet them all on the way down again". Believe me, there's never so much truth in a saying. I had to knock on a lot of doors looking for work after Boyzone ended. I met all the same people that I'd met while we'd been in the band. If I had been behaving like an ass, it would have made things very difficult when it was all over!

'And always remember your roots. Don't forget where you came from. Some people want to forget where they came from, but they should think about the values they had before they were famous or successful. You should step back every so often and really think back to your life before you had the fame, the money, the nice cars. Then see if you like the person you've become. You should constantly evaluate and assess your life and see if you're moving in the right direction. I've had to call myself up. I noticed that I was getting a little bit arrogant, behaving just a little bit short with people, and I had to ask myself "would I like to be treated like that?" I had to admit that I probably wouldn't. So I tried to change. I find being a nicer person makes me a happier one anyway.

'Also stay true to yourself. If you start doing well, you'll suddenly find a lot of hangers-on. Lots of people like to be around celebrities. Some hope to benefit financially. Some just want to be seen with the right people. Be aware of those people. You don't have to get rid of them, but just be aware of them. They are the ones who will tell you how great you are. They'll tell you that jacket looks great or that hairstyle looks great when it's rubbish. Keep those brown noses at bay or remember why they're there. Don't let them replace the real people in your life – the ones who are always there for you and the ones who will say what they really think.

'Success and fame change everyone; you should do your best to try and make sure those changes are positive ones.'

FIRST, I'D LIKE to thank Elton John, David Bowie, Dusty Springfield, Marvin Gaye and Patsy Cline for all the great music. In grateful thanks too to Brian Epstein and John Reid for being great managers and *NME*, *Smash Hits* and *Top of the Pops* for all the great memories.

I'd really like to thank all the people and good friends who generously gave their time and expertise to help me with this book including John Reynolds, Linda Martin, Peter Aiken, Colin Barlow, Alan McEvoy, Dave Bell, Barry Gastor, Caroline McAteer, Yvie Burnett, Paul Higgins, Priscilla Samuels, Keith Duffy, Kian Egan, Mags Humphries, Gary Kavanagh, Paul Kramer and Carol Hannah.

I'd also like to thank some other very significant people in my life including my absolutely fabulous friend Sharon Osbourne who kindly agreed to write the foreword for this book. Plus, of course, her right hand women, Sylvana Arena and Lynn Seager and her wonderfully bold daughter, Kelly.

Thanks also to Simon Cowell for being there; to Richard Holloway for hiring, firing and re-hiring me, and all the real stars of *X Factor*, Claire Horton, Andrew Llinares, Ben Thursby and Sara Lee.

I'd like to thank Lucian Grainge for lots of words of wisdom and fine cars, and David Joseph and Colin Barlow in the home of hits. Also thanks to Sonny Taghar and Dan Parker at Syco.

Thanks also to my great agent Heather Holden-Brown and to Doug, Larry, Bill, Martin, Ed, Alison, Janine, Vivien, Sheila and Simon and all the guys at Transworld. Thanks for your help, support and belief in this book.

Of course, I have to thank the Walsh family in Kiltimagh for putting up with me and more friends including all the great guys of Westlife and Boyzone, Shayne Ward, Caroline Desmond, Desmond Morris, Paul McGuinness, Johnny Logan, Tommy Hayden and the man who gave me a start in this business, Doc Carroll, who is now part of the big silver juke box in the sky.

And I'd like to thank the parish priest for the loan of the hall.